Ma

MAHARISHI
UNIVERSITY OF
MANAGEMENT

Wholeness
on the move

*His Holiness
Maharishi Mahesh Yogi*

who introduced Transcendental Meditation thirty-eight years ago and brought enlightenment to millions of people in the world, is now bringing the knowledge of Natural Law to the field of Management.

*M*y University of Management will create managers who will float in happiness, success, and fulfilment. They will command authority in the field of progress and dictate their terms to the environment.

They will be the guiding light of the post-industrial era, and functioning through Nature's Principle of Least Action, initiating dynamism in silence, they will introduce automation in administration to create a stable, balanced economy.

They will be the embodiment of positivity and harmony, in whose presence nothing can go wrong, and will raise management to a new, enlightened level of performance, which will nourish everyone and everything.

They will bring the dawn of new fortune to any field they choose to lead and will usher in a prosperous, blissful time of progress, peace, and fulfilment in all fields of business management and public administration.

—Maharishi

Maharishi University of Management

TABLE OF CONTENTS

Maharishi's Master Management
Engaging the Managing Intelligence of Natural Law 8

Managing Intelligence of Nature 19

Absolute Management
Origin of Law and its Evolution
Mechanics of One Becoming Many 35

Application of Law
Training to Avoid Problems and Failures 74

Timely Management TM
Maharishi's Master Management
is TIMELY MANAGEMENT
MMM is TM 79

Fundamental of Management
WHOLENESS 85

Supreme Management
Move of WHOLENESS 95

Broad Comprehension and
Ability to Focus Sharply **106**

The Science and Art of Management
Purity of Life Is the Basis of Success **108**

The Goal of Maharishi
University of Management **112**

Importance of Culture
*Spontaneous Application of
Natural Law to Management* **115**

Parental Role of Management **119**

Natural Law, Cosmic Manager of
the Universe, Invincible Source of
Order and Harmony Discovered
in the Human Physiology **123**

Supreme Quality of Management
Action from the Settled State of Mind **170**

Transcendental Meditation **174**

- Transcendental Meditation
  The Promoter of Evolution. **178**

- Transcendental Meditation
  Enjoyable Exercise of
  Vedic Mathematics **180**

TM-Sidhi Programme **185**

Yogic Flying **185**

- EEG Research Locates the Seat of Perfect Management in the Human Brain through the TM-Sidhi Programme of Yogic Flying **186**

Maharishi Effect **190**

The Extended Maharishi Effect **192**

Global Maharishi Effect **193**

Scientific Research on Transcendental Meditation, the TM-Sidhi Programme, and Yogic Flying in the Field of Management **197**

Neurophysiology of Creativity
A Calm, Collected Mind Is the Fountain-head of Creativity **204**

- Improved Brain Function—Skill in Activity **211**
- Deep Rest and Increasing Order—the Third Law of Thermodynamics: an Analogy from Physical Science ... **214**
- Innovative Thinking—Channeling Creativity for Accomplishment **218**

Creativity in Management Training **219**

Maharishi's Master Management
and Job Satisfaction in Business,
Industry, and Civil Service **222**

Maharishi's Vedic Management
*The Complete Science and
Technology of Management* **225**

Cry for Help **236**

- Successful Founders
  of Family Industries **243**

Turn Around **249**

Enlightenment and Fulfilment
in Management **331**

Invitation **335**

Maharishi's Achievements
*A Glimpse of Thirty-Eight Years
Around the World, 1957–1995* **336**

Visual Display of Maharishi's
Master Management **340**

*Here is the expression of supreme
knowledge in Maharishi's own words*

8

Maharishi's Master Management
*Engaging the Managing
Intelligence of Natural Law*

Maharishi's Master Management (MMM) is the supreme system of management. It introduces the organizing power of Natural Law into the fabrics of every area of management. (Refer to pages 22–24.)

The organizing power of Natural Law is that infinite organizing power which sustains existence and promotes the evolution of everything in the universe, automatically maintaining the well coordinated relationship of everything with everything else.

Maharishi's Master Management maintains the managing intelligence of the manager in alliance with this supreme managing intelligence of the universe, and thereby renders his administration as automatic, problem-free, ever-progressive, and ever-evolutionary as the administration of the universe through Natural Law.

Maharishi's Master Management trains the manager to take a stand in the science and art of management through Natural Law, and thereby brings the support of Natural Law to every aspect of management, nourishing and supporting the evolution of every area in the whole range

Manager in his stable, self-referral consciousness

The infinite organizing power of Natural Law, through its lively, quiet presence (catalytic agent) in every point of creation spontaneously radiates the infinite organizing power of self-referral dynamism, and this is how the all-directional performance of the manager spontaneously achieves maximum results in a natural way through minimum effort.

of the manager's concern, so that he enjoys the constant growth of the company, fulfilling the supreme goal of management—prosperity, progress, fulfilment, success, and peace—for himself and for all concerned.

Maharishi University of Management trains managers to achieve this supreme level of management characterized by AUTOMATION IN ADMINISTRATION.

Training in management at Maharishi University of Management offers a unique approach to perfect management. It shields the manager and his management from going out of BALANCE.

The comprehensive success and achievement of the manager is possible by virtue of the all-directional performance of Natural Law, which works for him by virtue of his fully awake, fully alert, self-referral consciousness—the level of the total creative potential of Natural Law, the greatest, most complete administration, which governs the ever-evolving, ever-progressive universe with perfect precision and order.

It is the discovery of the all-encompassing performance of the holistic value of Natural Law in the performance of individual Laws of Nature; and it is the discovery of the technology to align individual awareness with this level of Nature's Intelligence; and it is the performance of indi-

The supreme manager awake and alert in the scintillating intelligence of every grain of creation—the absolute administrator displaying precision and order in the ever-expanding universe.

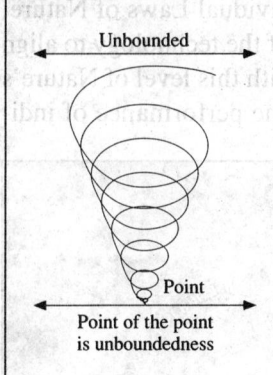

Illustration of the principle of the mechanics of administration through Natural Law: how, like a whirlpool, Natural Law manages all interests on the surface from one single point at its base, to which all activity converges and from where all activity emerges.

vidual, specific values of different Laws of Nature from one single awareness that is at the basis of Maharishi's Master Management (MMM), which has emerged to eliminate the problems of management in the world (1995).

Managing directors of companies and their executives are invited to take full advantage of the establishment of Maharishi University of Management.

---

* This level of reality is available to everyone in his own Transcendental Consciousness, where consciousness is fully awake in its pure wakefulness—
Continued on page 270 ...

As the skill of management has its focal point in the Principle of Least*Action, practical knowledge of this level of perfect management must be the basic requirement of training in management.

All areas of management that are being attended to by the institutes of management throughout the world simply lack management through Natural Law, which utilizes the Principle of Least Action to accomplish maximum with minimum effort.

Training in the holistic value of management along with training in specific areas of management will make management really complete and effective.

Specific areas of management training prevalent in institutes of management in the world are:

- **Financial Management and Accounting**
    – Financial Accounting
    – Managerial Accounting

---

* Natural Law functions through the Principle of Least Action.

This means that the orderly dynamics of Nature is
Continued on page 271 ...

- Financial Management

- **Legal and Economic Environment of Business**
  - Business Economics: Micro-economics
  - Business Economics: Macro-economics
  - Legal Environment of Business

- **Operations Management and Information Technology**
  - Production and Operations Management
  - Management Information Systems
  - Data Analysis for Decision-Making

- **Organizational Behaviour**
  - Human Resource Management
  - Behaviour in Organizations

- **Business Development and Strategy**
  - Marketing Management
  - Strategic Management and Change
  - Leadership and Entrepreneurship

- **International Management**
  - International Business
  - Cross-Cultural Management

All these areas of management that are generally taught in management institutes in the world today are also taught in Maharishi University of Management with the additional feature of the knowledge* of Natural Law—the knowledge and experience of consciousness—to enliven the total creative potential of these areas of management and management as a whole in the awareness of the manager, in his own consciousness, and in the collective consciousness of all the people involved with him in management—all those officers or workers involved within the range of his management.

Including the infinite organizing power of Natural Law in his management, within the range of his own authority, he will bring the collective consciousness of his company in alliance with Natural Law, and will open a new gate of fortune for peace, prosperity, and progress to be enjoyed by all, and achieve automation in administration.

In the field of management both things

---

* Principles of Success from Maharishi's Natural Law-Based Management; Full Development of the Individual, Organization, and Society.

have to be included: the physiology part of it—the tools, techniques, and systems (financing, banking, etc.)—and along with the consideration of all these, the element of intelligence—the inner intelligence within each of these.

Management is a highly sophisticated technology, therefore both these values—intelligence and its expressions—must be considered; and because it is the inner, pure intelligence that has expressed itself in the outer structures, for the development of the technology of management the field of intelligence should be given primary importance.

Maharishi University of Management handles management from the field of intelligence, and for the sake of intellectual satisfaction, the systems and tools, such as financing, banking, accounting, etc., are also considered.

Training in management at Maharishi University of Management is truly a training in Master

Management, and is called Maharishi's Master Management because it has been designed to maintain the supreme dignity of the science and art of management so that it can really actualize the meaning of the word 'management', which should have the ability to successfully achieve the target without stress and strain.

Maharishi's Master Management will protect MANAGEMENT from drifting into mis-management.

All institutions of management are invited to feel at home with Maharishi University of Management, and all the renowned experts of management are cordially invited to examine this programme of Maharishi's Master Management in the national and international conferences that will be organized by Maharishi Universities (or Maharishi Institutes or Maharishi Schools) of Management in different parts of the world, in collaboration with other institutes of management in different countries, including China, India, Russia, the U.S.A., and Japan.

Problems exist in all fields of human concern, including politics, economics, health, education,

Continued on page 19 …

18

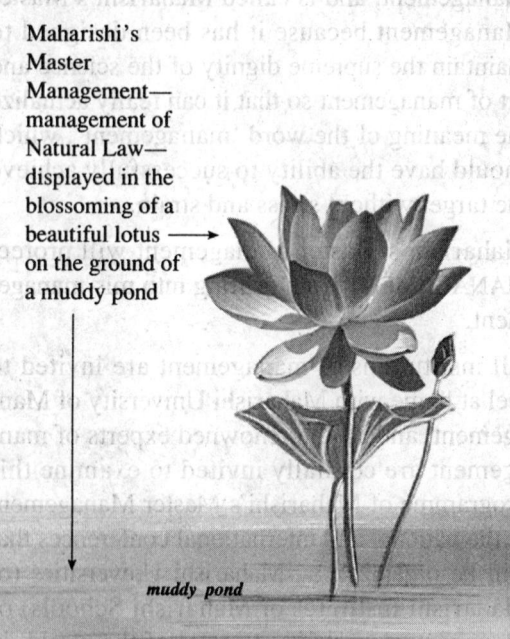

Maharishi's Master Management—management of Natural Law—displayed in the blossoming of a beautiful lotus on the ground of a muddy pond

muddy pond

Management in the world today is exemplified by a muddy pond—problems resulting from the prevailing systems of management, which are devoid of the nourishing, evolutionary influence of Natural Law.

agriculture, and industry in varying degrees of intensity in almost every country. In the presence of problems—in the problem-ridden society—freedom, progress, and defence are always a question mark for any sovereign nation. Life in the world has drifted away from its natural path of evolution; the result is that man continues to struggle through problems, and management, instead of promoting waves of success, struggles to solve problems. What was needed is a new era in management and Maharishi's Master Management has provided it.

The establishment of Maharishi Universities, Colleges, and Schools of Management in every country will be a new bright star for human destiny, and will create a problem-free society, and usher in the dawn of Heaven on Earth.

Managing Intelligence of Nature

The advantage of maintaining the liveliness of Natural Law in the awareness of the manager is that the holistic value of Natural Law and the specific values of different Laws of Nature spontaneously remain lively in the manager's emotions, his thoughts, his logic, his decisions, and his behaviour—Natural Law gets spontaneously woven into the fabrics of all the different areas of the manager's concern (financing, marketing, etc.) and makes management really complete and effective. There is no shadow of weakness in the whole range of the manager's responsibility.

The following pages (21–24) should be carefully studied to actualize the full significance of this new, more comprehensive theme of management.

The total value of Natural Law, through its self-interacting dynamics, evolves into thirty-six qualities of Natural Law, the thirty-six modes of the holistic value of Natural Law. These are the thirty-six clusters of Natural Law, clusters of the holistic value of Natural Law—different specific systems, which basically inspire the activity of the self-referral holistic performance of Natural Law.

The thirty-six specific values of the non-specific wholeness of the self-referral state of Natural Law are the qualities of consciousness that are

Continued on page 25 ...

21

Figure I

Holistic value of Natural Law

specific values of different Laws of Nature

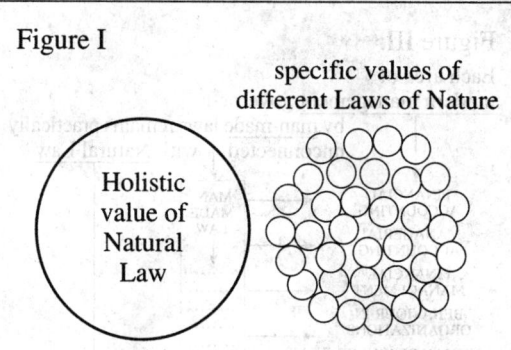

Figure II

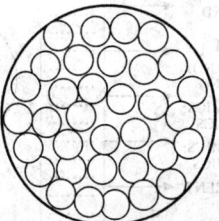

'Whole is more than the collection of parts'

This means that the holistic value of Natural Law maintains its own identity while upholding all the specific values of different Laws of Nature. (Refer to pages 85–106.)

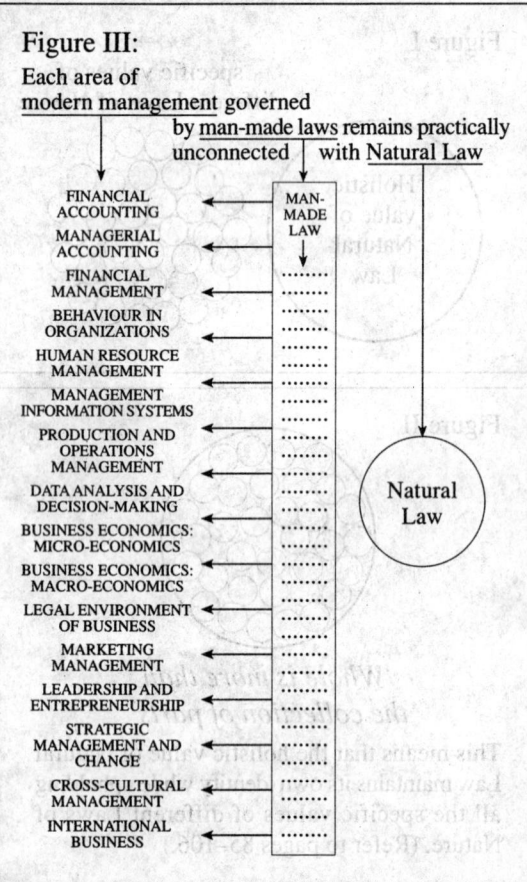

Figure IV

Maharishi's Master Management, enlivening the organizing power of the holistic value of Natural Law in the consciousness of the manager, directly infuses the infinite organizing power of Natural Law in man-made law, which governs each area of management.

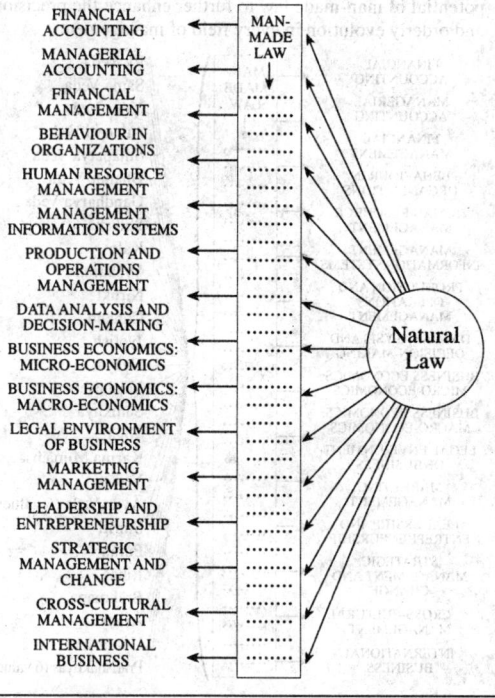

Figure V

Maharishi's Master Management, enlivening the organizing power of all the thirty-seven values of Natural Law (including the organizing power of specific values of their divisions and subdivisions) in the consciousness of the manager, directly enriches the influence of man-made law, and utilizes the total potential of man-made law to further enhance the precision and orderly evolution in every field of management.

	MAN-MADE LAW	
FINANCIAL ACCOUNTING	←	Ṛk Veda
MANAGERIAL ACCOUNTING	←	Sāma Veda
FINANCIAL MANAGEMENT	←	Yajur-Veda
BEHAVIOUR IN ORGANIZATIONS	←	Atharva Veda
HUMAN RESOURCE MANAGEMENT	←	Sthāpatya Veda
MANAGEMENT INFORMATION SYSTEMS	←	Dhanur-Veda
PRODUCTION AND OPERATIONS MANAGEMENT	←	Gandharva Veda
DATA ANALYSIS AND DECISION-MAKING	←	Shikshā
BUSINESS ECONOMICS: MICRO-ECONOMICS	←	Kalp
BUSINESS ECONOMICS: MACRO-ECONOMICS	←	Vyākaraṇ
LEGAL ENVIRONMENT OF BUSINESS	←	Nirukt
MARKETING MANAGEMENT	←	Chhand
LEADERSHIP AND ENTREPRENEURSHIP	←	Jyotish
STRATEGIC MANAGEMENT AND CHANGE	←	Nyāya
CROSS-CULTURAL MANAGEMENT	←	Vaisheshik
INTERNATIONAL BUSINESS	←	Sāmkhya
		Yoga
		Karma Mīmāṁsā
		Vedānt
		Āyur-Veda (6 values)
		Smṛiti
		Purāṇ
		Itihās
		Brāhmaṇa
		Āraṇyak
		Upanishad
		Prātishākhyas (6 values)

basic to creation and evolution—they are the structuring dynamics of the holistic value of Natural Law—the structure of Ṛk Veda.

Knowledge and experience of these thirty-seven[*] qualities of consciousness educates and thereby enlivens the ability of every individual to live perfection in life and enjoy the fruit of perfect management.

Maharishi University of Management brings to light the thirty-seven values of intelligence, the characteristic qualities of consciousness, which are fundamental to existence and evolution.

The following chart (pages 26–29) presents the thirty-seven qualities of Natural Law—the managing intelligence of Nature—and each quality expressed in the terminology of the Vedic Literature—the textbooks of Natural Law—and in the terminology of the physiology—the complete expression of Natural Law.

Continued on page 31 ...

---

[*] Holistic value = 1 (Ṛk Veda); specific qualities of the holistic value of Natural Law = 36 (the Vedic Literature). This is how 36 + 1 are expressed as the 37 qualities of Natural Law.

'MANAGING INTEL

Impulses of Consciousness—Structures a

their Qualities	*their Sound*	*their Form*
Qualities of Consciousness	Terminology of Vedic Literature	Terminology of Modern Physiology
holistic	Rk Veda	The whole physiology
flowing wakefulness	Sāma Veda	Sensory systems
dynamic and *creative*	Yajur-Veda	Processing systems
reverberating WHOLENESS	Atharva Veda	Motor systems
established in itself	Sthāpatya Veda	Anatomy
invincible and *progressive*	Dhanur-Veda	Immune system Biochemistry
integrating and *harmonizing*	Gandharva Veda	Cycles and Rhythms Pacemaker Cells
expression	Shikshā	Autonomic ganglia
transformation	Kalp	Limbic system
expansion	Vyākaran	Hypothalamus

'ENCE' OF NATURE
ructuring Dynamics of the Laws of Nature

Ref. pages 274–275

their Qualities	*their Sound*	*their Form*
Qualities of Consciousness ⇒	**Terminology of Vedic Literature** ⇒	**Terminology of Modern Physiology**
self-referral ⇒	Nirukt ⇒	Pituitary gland
measuring and *quantifying* ⇒	Chhand ⇒	Neurotransmitters, Neurohormones
all-knowing ⇒	Jyotish ⇒	Basal ganglia, Cerebral cortex, Cranial nerves, Brain stem
decisive and *distinguishing* ⇒	Nyāya ⇒	Thalamus
specific ⇒	Vaisheshik ⇒	Cerebellum
enumerating ⇒	Sāṁkhya ⇒	Types of neuronal activity
unifying ⇒	Yoga ⇒	Association fibres
analysing ⇒	Karma Mīmāṁsā ⇒	12 divisions of central nervous system
I-ness or *Being* ⇒	Vedānt ⇒	Integrated functioning of central nervous system

continues ...

Qualities of Consciousness ⇨	Terminology of Vedic Literature ⇨	Terminology of Modern Physiology
holding together, *nourishing*, and *supporting*	Charak	Mesodermal tissues and organs
balancing	Sushrut	Endodermal tissues and organs
communicating and *eloquent*	Vāgbhatt	Ectodermal tissues and organs
enlightening	Bhāva-Prakāsh	Cell nucleus
synthesizing	Shārngadhar	Cytoplasm and Cytoskeleton
detecting and *recognizing*	Mādhav Nidān	Cell membrane
memory	Smṛiti	Memory systems and reflexes
ancient and *eternal*	Purāṇ	Great intermediate net
blossoming of Totality	Itihās	Voluntary motor and sensory projections
structuring	Brāhmaṇa	Descending tracts of central nervous system

Qualities of Consciousness	Terminology of Vedic Literature	Terminology of Modern Physiology
stirring	Āraṇyak	Fasciculi proprii
transcendental and *self-referral*	Upanishad	Ascending tracts of central nervous system
all-pervading	Ṛk Veda Prātishākhya	Plexiform layer —horizontal communication *Cerebral Cortex Layer 1*
silencing, *sharing*, and *spreading*	Shukl-Yajur-Veda Prātishākhya	Corticocortical fibres *Cerebral Cortex Layer 2*
omnipresent	Krishn-Yajur-Veda Prātishākhya *(Taittirīya)*	Commisural and Corticocortical fibres *Cerebral Cortex Layer 3*
unmanifesting the parts but *manifesting* the whole	Sāma Veda Prātishākhya *(Pushpa Sūtram)*	Thalamocortical fibres *Cerebral Cortex Layer 4*
unfolding	Atharva Veda Prātishākhya	Cortico-striate, -tectal, -spinal fibres *Cerebral Cortex Layer 5*
dissolving	Atharva Veda Prātishākhya *(Chaturadhyāyī)*	Corticothalamic, Corticoclaustral fibres *Cerebral Cortex Layer 6*

- one *holistic* value of Natural Law—Ṛk Veda

- 36 *specific* values of Natural Law—the structuring dynamics of Ṛk Veda as displayed in the Vedic Literature

- *divisions* of each of the 36 specific values of Natural Law

- *subdivisions* of each of the divisions of the 36 specific values of Natural Law

This shows that everyone on the level of his self-referral consciousness is lively in all the thirty-seven clusters of the managing intelligence of Natural Law. Every aspect of the human physiology is an expression of this inner intelligence, and therefore every individual (mind and body) is a complete expression of the managing intelligence of Nature.

Let us now consider the relationship between different values of Natural Law—different values of the managing intelligence of Nature—on the practical level of the hierarchy of management.

<u>It is interesting to observe</u> that the holistic value of Natural Law has its seat in the *ĀTMĀ* (Self) of everyone, the self-referral intelligence of everyone—the unified level of Natural Law,* the level of that holistic value of Natural Law which is more than the collected value of all the (thirty-six) parts of Natural Law.+

<u>It is further interesting to observe</u> that these

---

* Refer to page 274.
+ Refer to page 275.

thirty-six specific parts of Natural Law are the functioning intelligence of Nature, which have their seat in the INTELLECT.

It is still further interesting to observe that the divisions of each of these thirty-six specific values of the holistic value of Natural Law have their common seat in the field of the MIND.

It is still even more interesting to observe that the subdivisions of each division of the thirty-six specific values of the holistic value of Natural Law have their seat in the field of the SENSES.

SELF (*Ātmā*)
↓
INTELLECT (*Buddhi*)
↓
MIND (*Manas*)
↓
SENSES (*Indriyas*)

It is important to note that each of these levels of consciousness, or intelligence—Self (*Ātmā*), intellect (*Buddhi*), mind (*Manas*), senses (*Indriyas*)—have their own corresponding level of physiology. (Refer to pages 130–131.)

This presents the hierarchy of the managing intelligence of Nature evolving from one holistic value to innumerable differentiated values of Natural Law, each value of Natural Law managing its corresponding level of evolution or progress while maintaining at its basis the total wakefulness of the holistic value of Natural Law — the common basis of all the different Laws of Nature.

It is interesting to see that the holistic level of intelligence of Natural Law corresponds with the holistically, ever-expanding physiology of the universe, and different structuring dynamics of this holistic value correspond with different levels of the physiology of the universe—the management of galaxies, solar systems, and planets, coming down to different countries in our world.

All these different areas of knowledge and their implications constitute the grand theory of management and its application.

Maharishi University of Management presents a complete theme of perfect management directly based on the supreme managing intelligence of Nature.

The teaching of banking, accounting, etc., in all

the existing institutes of management in the world does not include the element of Natural Law which, being the total potential of the organizing power in Nature, is the managing intelligence of Nature at the basis of all specific streams of knowledge that co-ordinates all the different values of management, supporting all the SPECIFIC areas of management from their common basis in the HOLISTIC potential of management.

This transforms the common knowledge of banking, auditing, etc., into knowledge that belongs to perfect management—Maharishi's Master Management.

Absolute Management
Origin of Law and Its Evolution
Mechanics of One Becoming Many

Law is that which manages. Law is that which is meant to manage—Law is management. Law is that binding force which maintains order. Law is that which is order in its stru*cture and func*-

---

* Refer to the discovery of the structures and func-
Continued ...

tion. Law is organizing power. Law is that which guides management and makes management progressive. Law is that which maintains the fulfilling nature of management. Law is that which maintains progress. Law is that which maintains fulfilling progress. Law is that which is the basis of everything. Law is that which is the basis of everything, whether unmanifest WHOLENESS or the expression of unmanifest WHOLENESS—the universe. Law is that which maintains WHOLENESS eternally in its self-referral state and makes the steady state of WHOLENESS move within itself. Law is that which maintains the moving quality in the unmoving quality of WHOLENESS. Law is that invincible binding force which maintains the existence and evolution of everything through its moving and unmoving, self-referral nature.

It is extremely useful and enlightening to under-

Footnote continues ...
tions of Law—structures and functions of intelligence—at the basis of the physiology, at the basis of creation, and at the basis of the eternal order in the infinite diversity of the ever-expanding, ever-evolving universe, pages 123–169.

stand this seemingly contradictory nature of Law (which is both moving and unmoving), because only in the coexistence of absolutely contradictory values can absolute balance, absolute order, absolute self-sufficiency, absolute organizing power, absolute existence, and absolute evolution be sustained. Law is the sustainer of everything; Law is the maintainer of everything; Law is the promoter of the progress, or evolution, of everything.

Knowledge of the origin and evolution of Law will give us the knowledge of everything. Knowledge of everything means the knowledge of all values—unifying and diversifying—including the knowledge of the transformation of unifying values into diversifying values, and diversifying values into unifying values. Knowledge of Law will give us custody, or authority, over order and its ordering mechanics. Knowledge of Law will give us the infinite organizing power of Law. Knowledge of Law will give us all possibilities in the field of impossibilities; it will give us perfe*ction, infinite organizing power, infinite

---

* This knowledge comes to bring fulfilment to the
Continued ...

managing power in the field of management.

This will give us total command over the field of management so that nothing will remain out of the authority of management; everything will always remain within the absolute Law of management, which is always the field of all possibilities, the field of WHOLENESS—the field of WHOLENESS on the move within itself.

Here is the origin of Law. Here is the origin of Law in the nature of WHOLENESS—in the move of WHOLENESS within itself.

> The origin of Law is visible in the move of WHOLENESS;
> the origin of Law is visible in the move of WHOLENESS;
> **the origin of Law is visible in the move of WHOLENESS.**

Footnote continues ...
'paradigm shift' from more concrete (banking, accounting, etc.) to more abstract, but more fundamentally effective values of management (Vedic Management), based on the knowledge and experience of the mechanics of transformation of Law in the field of consciousness.

The origin of Law is visible not only in the move of WHOLENESS, but also in the very steady state of WHOLENESS, from where WHOLENESS gains the inspiration and vitality to move.

Because the origin of Law is available in the nature of the self-referral move of WHOLENESS, the entire evolution of Law is visible in the origin of Law—the origin and evolution of Law are visible in the move of WHOLENESS.

We can visualize the origin of Law either in the self-referral WHOLENESS of silence or in the self-referral WHOLENESS of dynamism; we can visualize the origin of Law in the nature of WHOLENESS, which is both silence and dynamism at the same time; or, if we like, we can visualize the origin of Law sandwiched between the WHOLENESS of silence and the WHOLENESS of dynamism; in this way we can see the origin of Law in the self-referral, self-interacting dynamics of WHOLENESS, or Unity—the Ultimate Reality.

This vision of the origin and evolution of Law as the Ultimate Reality is the disclosure of the supreme power of Natural Law—the liveliness of the infinite organizing power of Natural Law—within the self-referral state of everyone's consciousness.

The origin and evolution of Law is lively in the self-referral dynamics of the Ultimate Reality, the field of self-referral consciousness. The custody of the total field of Law is lively in the field of the self-referral consciousness of everyone—the Absolute Manager is eternally lively, fully awake and fully alert, within the self-referral consciousness of everyone.

Law is the very nature of WHOLENESS. We can visualize Law upholding the silent nature of WHOLENESS, and we can also visualize Law upholding the move of WHOLENESS within itself — dynamism within the silent nature of WHOLENESS.

In this picture of Law we have the unmoving, or non-moving silent nature of Law, and the moving dynamic nature of Law; we see the structure of Law built in its own two values, silence and

---

* Access to this level of Law is now being made available to everyone through Maharishi's Master Management. (Refer to pages 9–11.)

dynamism, and silence and dynamism available in the move of WHOLENESS.

So the total quality of Law is the quality of 'silence on the move' — the silent structure of Law and the dynamic structure of Law both together constituting the move of WHOLENESS—WHOLENESS of Law on the move in the move of WHOLENESS.

Law equates with WHOLENESS. Silent Law equates with the steady state of WHOLENESS, and the dynamic structure of Law equates with the move of WHOLENESS. Even though the move of WHOLENESS is within the nature of WHOLENESS, nevertheless the move is a dynamic quality, and this expression of Law, this dynamic structure of WHOLENESS, presents the dynamic nature of Law on the ground of the silent nature of Law.

Thus, in the silent state of WHOLENESS, Law is established in itself; it is the self-referral state of Law. In its self-referral state, how Law behaves with itself is the fundamental dynamics of Law.

In the silent state of WHOLENESS, what are the

mechanics that inspire the self-referral, ultimate state of reality in Unity to flow out or flow in to create the dynamics of Law—the move of WHOLENESS?

In the move of silence, the move is there but it is the move of silent WHOLENESS. The mechanics that render silent Law to move within itself, still maintaining its silent quality, are the seat of the origin of Law, which is the seat of the evolution of Law, and now it is our joy to envision the mechanics of this origin and evolution of Law—the expression of the holistic, self-referral quality of Law.

Having clearly comprehended WHOLENESS in terms of Law—having clearly comprehended Law in terms of WHOLENESS—in the unfoldment of the mechanics of its evolution we will appreciate the whole range of its expression in terms of the ever-expanding universe.

Let us visualize or examine what Law does to itself; how Law behaves with itself in its self-referral state, the field of WHOLENESS. Let us see how the frozen value of Law, in its eternally silent structure, breathes life and maintains the liveliness—flow—of its silent WHOLENESS.

This area of knowledge is not only interesting and fascinating on the level of intellectual understanding, but it is highly useful on the practical level to achieve* anything.

We have seen that

    WHOLENESS equates with Law:

                        WHOLENESS = Law
     WHOLENESS awake within itself = Law
            self-referral WHOLENESS = Law
            self-referral wakefulness = Law
                  self-referral move = Law
                self-referral dynamism = Law
                  self-referral silence = Law
         togetherness of silence and
     dynamism (in WHOLENESS) = Law
              the move (dynamism)
          of WHOLENESS (silence) = Law
         the move of WHOLENESS
             dynamism of silence = Law

---

* As everything is the expression of Law, the evolution of everything is through the instrumentality of Law.

43

The self-referral state of WHOLENESS is the self-referral state of Law.

The expression 'self-referral WHOLENESS' means that WHOLENESS knows itself and nothing else—it is fully awake within itself—it is wakefulness. When we say 'self-referral Law' it means that Law knows itself and nothing else—it is fully awake within itself—it is wakefulness. This quality of wakefulness is the silent state of Law, which is fully awake within itself. It is actually not *awake within itself, **it is wakefulness itself**.

Law is wakefulness; wakefulness is WHOLENESS. WHOLENESS in its wakefulness is Law, fully awake within itself. WHOLENESS, or Law, fully awake within itself, fully knows itself. Knowing itself, it is the knower, the process of knowing, and the known; it is all three together in one WHOLENESS—it is the togetherness of three. In Vedic⁺ terms, it is called Saṁhitā (to-

---

* He who is awake is not separate from wakefulness. Law in its self-referral state of wakefulness is the
Continued on page 276 …

⁺ Language of Nature. (Refer to pages 123–169.)

getherness of three* qualities) of Ṛishi (knower), Devatā (process of knowing), and Chhandas (the known). The togetherness of knower, knowing, and known is the togetherness of subjectivity, objectivity, and their relationship, which covers the whole, infinitely diversified field of Law—the whole universe.

This total structure of Law is called the structure of pure knowledge—Ṛk Veda. Ṛk Veda, the total potential of Natural Law, being the total structure of Natural Law, is obviously the total Constitution of Natural Law—the lively+ Constitution of the Universe within the self-referral consciousness of everyone.

Here is the vision of the dynamics of Law—the dynamics of the WHOLENESS of Law—the dynamics of the state of Law in Unity.

The origin of Law is Law itself.

Law equates with Veda; Law = Veda.

---

* Bhagavad-Gītā, 2.45.

+ We are extremely proud and grateful, and the whole mankind is eternally indebted, to that special class of

Continued on page 277 ...

The dynamics of Law equates with the self-interacting dynamics of Veda; dynamics of Law = dynamics of Veda.

Structures of Law manifest as the structures of Ṛk Veda; structures of Law = structures of Ṛk Veda.

Structures of Law are available in the sounds of the Veda and Vedic Literature; structures of Law = sounds of the Veda and Vedic Literature.

Structures of Law manifest in the structures of speech; structures of Law = structures of speech (*Shruti*—that which is heard).

Structures of Law manifest as the sounds of the Vedic Literature, which continue to evolve into material particles forming the physiology and their modes of behaviour; structures of Law = physical*structures.

Thus, whatever is there on the level of speech or material creation is the expression of Law. That is why we see that everything is precise, and the relationship of everything with everything else in creation is orderly.

---

* Refer to pages 123–169.

Law is the ordering agency; and because it is managing its own reality, the order in the universe is eternal and infinite.

Law is the reality of everyone at every level of evolution. Everything is essentially the expression of Law. Law itself is the source of Law; Law itself is the course of Law; and Law itself is the goal of Law—Law is this, that, and everything. The expression 'everything is Law' means that the whole creation is the expression of Law.

This vision of Law is the vision of Veda; this structure of Law is the structure of Veda, which is the basis of all expressed creation. And where is this? In the self-interacting dynamics of pure wakefulness; and here, on the level of one's own self-referral consciousness, one can identify oneself with this enormous organizing power—the infinite organizing power of Natural Law; and from this level of mastery over oneself, mastery over Natural Law, the individual, the personification of Law, utilizes at will the wholeness of his unmanifest nature—the wholeness of Law, unmanifest Law.

Manifest Law uses its own unmanifest Law because the manifest is just the personification of the unpersonified, unmanifest WHOLENESS—unmanifest Law—unmanifest Veda—unmanifest Self.

In this picture, the ORIGIN of Law is the self-interacting dynamics of consciousness, and the EVOLUTION of Law is also in the self-interacting dynamics of consciousness, the sequence of evolution of the Veda and Vedic Literature.

The sequence of the evolution of Law is available in the sequence of the Vedic Structure as it sequentially evolves from beginning to end—from its first letter to its last letter, as available to us in the traditional recitation of the Veda.

The mechanics of transformation of one structure of Law into another structure of Law in the sequence* of the unfoldment of Ṛk Veda presents a very beautiful vision of the mechanics of the evolution of Law as its structure evolves from its unmanifest state to its manifest state—from the unmanifest state of intelligence to the specific structures of intelligence.

---

*Refer to Maharishi's *Apaurusheya Bhāshya* of Ṛk Veda—Lesson Ten of Maharishi's Vedic Science.

The dynamics of Law, the dynamics of the self-referral, holistic value of Law—the dynamics of Unity—present two perspectives:

1. The move of Unity as Unity; the move of WHOLENESS as WHOLENESS; the move of Law as Law;

2. The dynamics of Unity quietly initiating the process of the diversification of Unity; the dynamics of WHOLENESS quietly initiating the process of the diversification of WHOLENESS; the dynamics of Law quietly initiating the process of the diversification of Law.

In this perspective, two qualities of Law are seen in their state of togetherness. This means that the total value of Law maintains two characteristics in its nature—the tendency to maintain its state of Unity and the tendency to move in the direction of diversity—the tendency to maintain WHOLENESS and make WHOLENESS move—the tendency to present WHOLENESS in parts—the tendency of the holistic value of Law to spontaneously diversify itself into the structure of different Laws of Nature.

This is Natural Law, which is fully equipped

within itself to operate through its own self-interacting dynamics.

Lively within this self-referral structure of Law is all that is needed for precision, mathematical precision and order, to display infinite order in the whole range of evolution—the evolution of one into many—the evolution of one, without*losing itself (WHOLENESS), in the process of becoming many—WHOLENESS on the move—the display of Law, the display of Absolute Management.

The word 'Absolute' indicates that this structure of management is indestructible; it is eternally indestructible; it is eternally the same, because it is Totality itself; it is the nature of Unity — the performer, his performance, the equipment, the tools, the processes, the systems are all lively, each in its totality, all within the WHOLENESS of Unity—the indestructible, inexhaustible structure of management—self-induced, self-perpetuating, self-sufficient—the field of all possibilities—the absolute, lively

---

* Refer to my Mathematics of the Absolute Number in my Absolute Theory of Management.

structure of Law—the infinite organizing power of Law—the self-referral field of knowledge—the Unified Field of the knower, knowing, and known—in the Vedic Language, 'Saṁhitā of Ṛishi, Devatā, Chhandas', Ṛk Veda—the total structure of Law—the absolute state of Law—eternal Law—the Law that is the Creator itself, and evolves*creation from within itself as its own image.

This nature of Natural Law, creating creation within its self-interacting dynamics—the Creator creating creation in its own image—is meaningful on that level of understanding that sees the structure of total Natural Law available in terms of its evolutionary nature—thirty-six values of WHOLENESS, the thirty-six qualities of self-referral intelligence—the structuring dynamics of Natural Law available in the thirty-

---

* तत्सृष्ट्वा तदेवानुप्राविशत्
Tat sṛishtwā tad evānuprāvishat
   (Taittirīya Upanishad, 2.6.2)
Having created the creation, the Creater entered into it.

Refer to the structure of Law at the basis of the physiology, pages 123–169.

six structures and corresponding functions of the human*physiology.

The picture is of one Law becoming many—one becoming many. Actually the relationship is lack of relationship, because one is many, one itself is many, not that one becomes many. The reality is that one is always many—the eternal one is eternally the many—it itself is the process of becoming; it itself is the field of Being, the eternal state of self-referral wakefulness—pure knowledge, the Veda, and the infinite organizing power of Veda available as the structuring dynamics of the Veda—Law, Natural Law, available as the sounds of the Veda and Vedic Literature.

Evolution is the absolute reality of creation—parts[+] evolve into parts and whole[⊕] evolves into

---

* Refer to 'Natural Law, Cosmic Manager of the Universe, Invincible Source of Order and Harmony Discovered in the Human Physiology', pages 123–169.

[+] The field of modern Mathematics of natural numbers.

[⊕] The field of my Vedic Mathematics of the Absolute Number.

whole. Simultaneity of evolution of parts and whole and the eternal continuum of this process of evolution is not random; it is orderly, it is eternally orderly; it is precise, it is eternally precise—it is the expression of Law.

The whole creation, the entire ever-expanding universe, is the expression of LAW that upholds ORDER—order in constancy and order in change—order in unity and order in diversity.

Law is studied by all disciplines of modern science through their objective approach. This objective approach to the knowledge of Law has made scientists familiar with the behaviour of specific Laws, but without familiarity with the holistic[*] value of Law and its intimate relationship with all specific[*] values of Law, and without this total value of Law lively within the awareness of the knower, the advantage of the total value of Law will not be available to the knower

---

* ऋक् (Rk) is the expression for Law in the Vedic Language.

+ It is my joy to acknowledge and appreciate the discoveries of the objective approach of modern science—the discovery of the Unified Field of all the

Continued on page 279 …

of Law, and Law will not become a living reality of daily life—life will not be spontaneously lived in full accord with Natural Law—the theme of progress will not rise to the level of the perfect theme of the evolution of Law, which is true for all time and place, and all situations and circumstances.

My Absolute Theory of Management offers familiarity with both values of Law, holistic and specific, so that the awareness of the manager remains awake in the total value of Law, so that the WHOLENESS of Law and individual, specific Laws play their separate roles in full accordance with each other, and the sequential process of evolution upholding every area of management is spontaneously maintained in all aspects of the manager's concern.*

Law, eternal Law, must be the living reality of everyone, because Law is the very basis of everyone's life; Law is the very essence of life; eternal

---

* Refer to my *Apaurusheya Bhāshya* of Ṛk Veda and to the discovery of Ṛk Veda and the structuring dynamics of Ṛk Veda, the Vedic Literature, in the human physiology.

Law, in its <u>holistic</u> value, is the total intelligence of total consciousness—self-referral consciousness—WHOLENESS.

How does this wholeness of Law become the specific values of Law? What are the dynamics of the emergence of Law? What are the dynamics of transformation of the WHOLENESS of Law into specific values of Law?

Knowledge of this is very necessary for everyone, because the reality of everyone's life is full of variety—the reality of any management is full of variety.

Every management is a complex network of many areas of management, and every area of management is a cluster of many principles and practices of management in itself. Thus we see that one wholeness of management contains within it many areas of management, and each area of management has its own holistic and specific values within it.

Knowledge of this is gained objectively through the disciplines of modern science, and subjectively through the different disciplines of my Vedic Science, which enlivens perfection in the field of management and offers automation in business management and public administration.

The WHOLENESS of Law appears in specific qualities of Law; but how does the WHOLENESS and specificity of Law together appear as the infinite diversity of creation, which is held in a unified state—Universe—the ever-expanding, ever-evolving universe?

This practical knowledge of Law is available in the qualities of intelligence that are inherent in the quality of WHOLENESS, and are expressed in the Language of Nature in which Law is expressed in its totality—the Vedic Language, which has been discovered as the language of intelligence: specific sounds, the sounds of the Veda, which reverberate as the structure of the DNA, the RNA, and the language of neurons, which altogether present the structures of Law

---

* For authenticity of this statement, refer to 'Natural Law, Cosmic Manager of the Universe, Invincible Source of Order and Harmony Discovered in the Human Physiology', pages 123–169.

✢ DNA is the executor of pure knowledge, expressed
Continued on page 284 …

and the functions of Law at the basis of the human physiology.

This practical knowledge of Law is available in the structure of intelligence—the structure of the Veda—which has its totality in the infinitely small concentrated point value and the most unbounded, ever-expanding value in the universe.* (Refer to pages 9 and 11.)

The sequential simultaneity of one and three (Saṁhitā of Ṛishi, Devatā, Chhandas) lays open the character of Law in the structure of Ṛk Veda—it is expanding and contracting at the same time; it is many and one at the same time.

Law, in its balancing nature, is displayed in the structure of Ṛk Veda and in its structuring dynamics, the Veda Literature.+

As one objectively and subjectively probes deeper into the nature of Law, one is only amazed with the display of its varying qualities, which emerge sequentially and simultaneously

---

* In the Vedic Expression: *Aṇoraṇīyān mahato mahīyān*—atom of the atom is bigger than the biggest,
Continued on page 285 ...

+ Refer to pages 130–131.

in such perfect precision that their symmetry and order is absolutely sustained at every moment and at all times.

For this symmetrical, balanced structure of Law, as available in the Veda and Vedic Literature, we refer to pages 130–131.

The symmetry and order of Law is most concentrated at a point and most expanded in the ever-expanding universe. The precision of Mathematics has its reality in this field of Law, the field of all possibilities, which is both point and infinity; it is sequential and simultaneous—it is the state of absolute balance. This is the essential characteristic quality of an administrator.

This absolutely balanced quality of Law is available in the structure of Ṛk Veda and its structuring dynamics, the Vedic Literature. The structure of Ṛk Veda and its structuring dynamics, the Vedic Literature, present this nature of balancing in the structure of Law.

The absolutely balanced, holistic value of Law expressed from the beginning to the end of Ṛk*

---

* Ṛk Veda of ten eternal structures—ten *Maṇḍals*.

Veda—the move of the wholeness of Law from the beginning to the end of Ṛk Veda—is beautifully illustrated in the sequential yet simultaneous activity of the thirty-six qualities of Law—the thirty-six qualities of intelligence—and their divisions and subdivisions, as available in the sounds of the Vedic Literature—the thirty-six names of the Vedic Literature.

The sound of each of the thirty-six values of the Vedic Literature is the name of a specific quality of Law, which in itself represents a cluster of different qualities, and each of these clusters represents further clusters of Natural Law.

The names of each of these thirty-six qualities of Law are the names of the structuring dynamics of Ṛk Veda; whereas Ṛk Veda presents the total structure of Law.

1. Ṛk Veda—*holistic*
2. Sāma Veda—*flowing wakefulness*
3. Yajur-Veda—*dynamic and creative*
4. Atharva Veda—*reverberating WHOLENESS*
5. Sthāpatya Veda—*established in itself*

6. Dhanur-Veda—*invincible and progressive*
7. Gandharva Veda—*integrating and harmonizing*
8. Shikshā—*expression*
9. Kalp—*transformation*
10. Vyākaraṇ—*expansion*
11. Nirukt—*self-referral*
12. Chhand—*measuring and quantifying*
13. Jyotish—*all-knowing*
14. Nyāya—*decisive and distinguishing*
15. Vaisheshik—*specific*
16. Sāṁkhya—*enumerating*
17. Yoga—*unifying*
18. Karma Mīmāṁsā—*analysing*
19. Vedānt—*I-ness or Being*
20. Charak—*holding together, nourishing, and supporting*
21. Sushrut—*balancing*
22. Vāgbhatt—*communicating and eloquent*

23. Bhāva-Prakāsh—*enlightening*
24. Shārngadhar—*synthesizing*
25. Mādhav Nidān—*detecting and recognizing*
26. Smṛiti—*memory*
27. Purāṇ—*ancient and eternal*
28. Itihās—*blossoming of Totality*
29. Brāhmaṇa—*structuring*
30. Āraṇyak—*stirring*
31. Upanishad—*transcendental and self-referral*
32. Ṛk Veda Prātishākhya—*all-pervading*
33. Shukl-Yajur-Veda Prātishākhya—*silencing, sharing, and spreading*
34. Kṛishṇ-Yajur-Veda Prātishākhya (*Taittirīya*)—*omnipresent*
35. Sāma Veda Prātishākhya (*Pushpa Sūtram*)—*unmanifesting the parts but manifesting the whole*
36. Atharva Veda Prātishākhya—*unfolding*
37. Atharva Veda Prātishākhya (*Chaturadhyāyi*)—*dissolving*

The above-mentioned individual qualities of intelligence each represent a cluster of qualities; that means each individual quality in itself represents an individual cluster, and each value of the cluster again, in itself, is a cluster of qualities. This total theme of the evolution of Law—Natural Law—is a three-step theme of evolution emerging from the three-step theme of evolution in the dynamics of WHOLENESS itself—Saṁhitā of Ṛishi, Devatā, Chhandas.

This three-step theme of evolution of Law emerges from within the nature of WHOLENESS, which expresses itself in terms of three qualities of WHOLENESS, three qualities of self-referral consciousness—subjectivity, objectivity, and the relationship of the two—because the self-referral structure of consciousness, being Unity, is all three values—it is the object of its own subject, and the relationship that connects subjectivity and objectivity (Saṁhitā of Ṛishi, Devatā, Chhandas).

On this level of the holistic value of Natural Law we have Ṛk Veda and sequentially evolving diverse values of Natural Law within the holistic value of Ṛk Veda.

A Vision of the Evolution of Natural Law in Three Steps—Move of WHOLENESS in Three Steps Following the First, Basic Three-Step Move of Ṛishi, Devatā, Chhandas Within the Nature of Saṁhitā

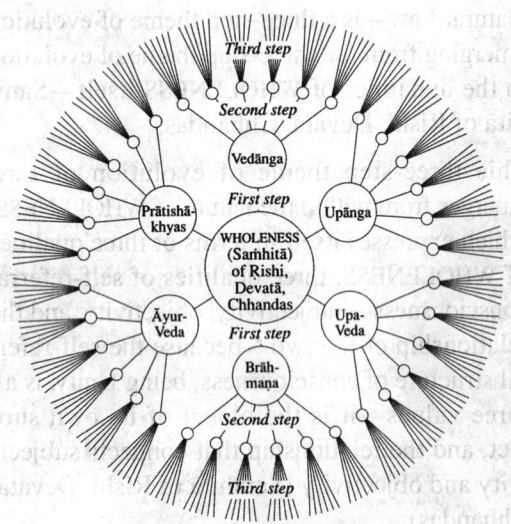

It is this symmetrical evolution of Natural Law that manifests in the orderly evolution of the ever-expanding universe.

This development of diverse values of Law within the unified value of WHOLENESS presents the mechanics of TRANSFORMATION of WHOLENESS into different values of WHOLENESS and lays open the world of WHOLENESS behaving with WHOLENESS — WHOLENESS functioning on its own eternal level of WHOLENESS.

In order to understand the mechanics of transformation of WHOLENESS into different values of WHOLENESS, we should look into the sequential evolution of Ṛk Veda and the structuring dynamics of this sequential evolution, which is available in the thirty-six areas of the Vedic Literature.

This aspect of knowledge presents a picture of how the thirty-six values of the structuring dynamics of Ṛk Veda, the thirty-six aspects of the Vedic Literature, function together.

The field of evolution displayed in the structure of the Veda and Vedic Literature is so profound and perfect that one could go on and on, ever unfolding the petals of this absolute field of knowledge. It is fulfilling on the academic level, and it is fulfilling on the level of its application in the practical field of life—the practical approach in the field of consciousness, in the field of Law, or in the field of technology.

The sequence of the evolution of the physiology follows the sequence of the evolution of the Vedic Structure—the sequence of the evolution of Ṛk Veda—the sequential evolution of Law evolving from the self-interacting dynamics of Unity, the wholeness of Law in its unified state.

This unified structure of Law spontaneously manifests into the sequentially evolving structure of the Veda, which in turn evolves in sequence into the structure of the physiology.

Perfection of management has its seat in unwaveringly following, spontaneously following, the sequence of the evolution of Law. Any little deviation, any side-tracking from the set theme of evolution, causes discomfort, stress, and strain to the natural, evolutionary direction of Law. Obstruction to the evolution of Natural Law is the cause of all stress, strain, problems, and suffering in life.

The treatise on the evolution of Natural Law, the Veda, is so beautifully complete and perfect, because it presents, with mathematical accuracy, the procedures of reverting back from the process of evolution so that the system can be repaired at the inception of any deviation of Law.

The knowledge and practical application of the thirty-*six values of Law, enumerated in the thirty-six values of the Vedic Literature and their divisions and subdivisions, is so perfect that, because their values are involved in structuring each aspect of the personality of everyone, there should be no chance for any aspect of anyone's life to deviate from the path of evolution.

Any violation of the evolution of Natural Law means violation of the sequential evolution of

---

* गहना कर्मणो गतिः
  Gahanā karmaṇo gatiḥ (Bhagavad-Gītā, 4.17)
  Unfathomable is the course of action.

When we say thirty-six, all thirty-six values are included in one holistic value (the thirty-seventh, Ṛk Veda); therefore, the divisions and subdivisions of all the clusters of the thirty-six are all involved in every activity and its evolution. That is why the course of any action is very complex.

Natural Law, as displayed in the sequential evolution of Ṛk Veda, and also in each of the thirty-six values of the Vedic Literature.

The natural direction of sequential evolution has its source on the level of memory, Smṛiti; therefore, correctional procedures are fully laid out in the Smṛiti, which cover the whole range of Law—all levels of the evolution of Law—all fields of sensory perception, mental perception, intellectual perception, and the self-referral perception on the level of the Self.

Knowledge of this origin and evolution of Law is perfect knowledge of life. Knowledge of this origin and evolution of Law is the absolute knowledge of life, and as any aspect of management is an aspect of the management of life, this knowledge of the origin and evolution of Law is

---

* There are eighteen Smṛiti—eighteen clusters of Natural Law within one grand cluster called Smṛiti (memory). These eighteen clusters of Natural Law appear in eighteen clusters of the physiology.

In physiological terms, these eighteen Smṛiti correspond to the eighteen nuclei of the cranial nerves with reference to the memory systems and reflexes. (Refer to page 157.)

the knowledge of Absolute Management.

Just to have a taste of the constituent qualities of this origin and evolution of Law, I wish to explain one of the thirty-six values of Natural Law called Shikshā, which presents the quality of EXPRESSION lively in the self-interacting dynamics of consciousness, the self-referral state of consciousness—the quality of EXPRESSION lively in the structure of Samhitā of Ṛishi, Devatā, Chhandas, the self-referral dynamics of Law—the dynamics of EXPRESSION—the dynamics of manifestation.

Study of Shikshā awakens or inspires the quality of EXPRESSION in the nature of pure intelligence. The quality of EXPRESSION is the most fundamental quality of consciousness at the basis of the creation and evolution of everything. It has its seat in the self-referral, self-sufficient nature of Unity Consciousness, in its state of eternal Unity, where the unified state of eternal Unity spontaneously expresses itself as Samhitā of Ṛishi, Devatā, Chhandas—the unified state of the knower, process of knowing, and known.

It is interesting and revealing to find the eternal

state of Unity (Saṁhitā) in terms of the quality* of EXPRESSION, which is at the basis of the appearance of the Ṛishi, Devatā, and Chhandas qualities in the nature of Saṁhitā.

The quality of EXPRESSION habituates intelligence, or consciousness, and its corresponding physiology, to flow sequentially in the natural evolutionary direction of Natural Law in such a way that the expressed value at every moment keeps realigning itself with its source—the field of pure intelligence, the fountain-head of Creative Intelligence—and thereby continuously revitalizes itself from this inexhaustible reservoir of energy and intelligence in the self-referral, unmanifest state of consciousness, maintaining an undisturbed, unrestricted, steady tempo⁺ of evolution.

---

* This quality of expression beautifully expresses itself in terms of six self-referral loops (refer to pages 130–131); it is the most fundamental quality of the Unity state of consciousness.

⁺ The process of evolution may be likened to the process of walking forward, which puts one step forward
Continued on page 286 ...

It is remarkable to see how the Vedānga* value of Shikshā remains aligned with the Veda value, the Samhitā value. The Samhitā value we have understood in terms of *Sandhi Samhitā*; that means Samhitā, or Veda, is the value lively in *Atyantābhāva* (absolute abstraction), and there, within the unmanifest nature of *Atyantābhāva*, is the fully alert, fully awake, all-directional openness of *Chitti Shakti*—the unified state of consciousness—the total potential of the Veda—the total potential of pure knowledge and its infinite organizing power, fully awake in its all-directional openness, all-directional wakefulness — fully alert, all-directional organizing power in the silent dynamism of *Anyonya-abhāva*—unmanifest WHOLENESS, fully alert to take any direction according to intention.

It is like standing on a crossing: one has a choice to take any direction. Alertness, fully awake within itself, is open in all 360°—all-directional,

Continued on page 71 ...

---

* *Anga*, the limb, is never separate from *Angi*, the body; Shikshā is never separate from Veda, because it is *Anga*, the limb of Veda, the body—Shikshā is never separate from Veda because it is Vedānga, the *Anga* of the Veda.

A Vision of the All-Directional, All-Dimensional Wakefulness of Natural Law—WHOLENESS Lively in Every Point of Its Expression

It is this fully alert, all-directional silent dynamism of the organizing power of Natural Law that upholds the orderly evolution of Natural Law expressed in the ever-expanding universe.

all-dimensional openness of the field of pure knowledge in silence, with its infinite organizing, dynamic power—the reservoir of the absolute potential of energy and intelligence—the natural process of the evolution of EXPRESSION (Shikshā quality of intelligence)—the vision of full alertness centred at a point in silence ready to move its focus in any direction, or any dimension, plans according to the intention.

This state of awareness* is only available in *Atyantābhāva*—absolute abstraction—the state of absolute alertness, fully awake in itself.

All the thirty-seven qualities of Natural Law have their source in the unmanifest WHOLENESS of *Atyantābhāva* and its lively organizing power, *Anyonyābhāva*. This is the point of transformation characterized by the absolute wakefulness of the holistic potential of Natural Law at the

Continued on page 74 ...

---

* Our stressed civilization is now destined to take a turn from action-predominant, chaotic, stressful, tiring management to silent-predominant, successful, healthy, holistic, natural management—management of the holistic wakefulness of Natural Law, which is management through the absolute alertness of the infinite organizing power of Natural Law.

A Vision of the Total
at the Junction Point Betwe

An Example from the First Verse of Ṛk Veda

Examples From All the Thirty-

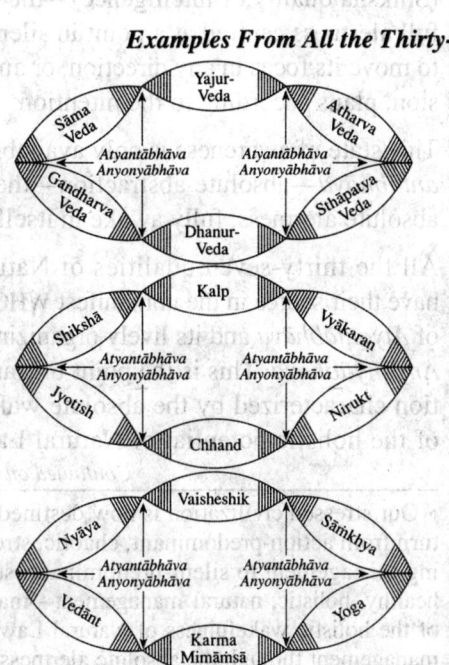

...tial of Natural Law
...ny Two of Its Expressions

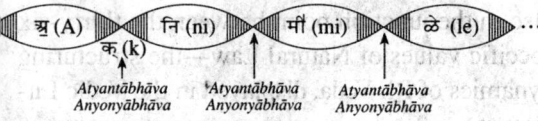

...lues of the Vedic Literature

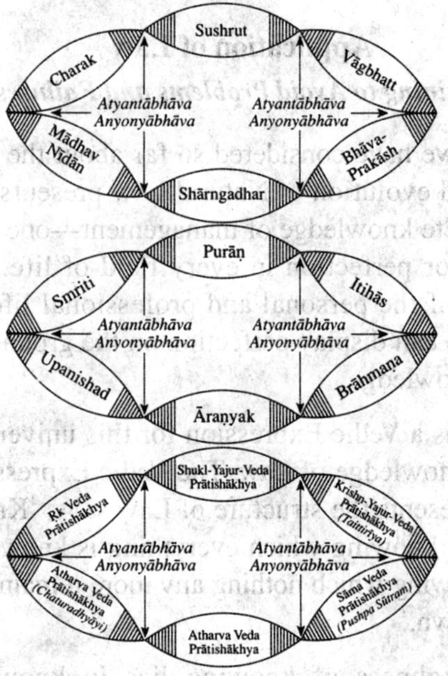

junction point (GAP) between any two expressions of the sequential progression of Natural Law, available in the structure of Ṛk Veda, and also in the junction point between the thirty-six specific values of Natural Law—the structuring dynamics of Ṛk Veda, displayed in the Vedic Literature.

Application of Law
Training to Avoid Problems and Failures

What we have considered so far about the origin and evolution of Natural Law presents the complete knowledge of management—one formula for perfection in every field of life. All fields of the personal and professional life of anyone can display perfection on the ground of this knowledge.

There is a Vedic Expression for this universal, total knowledge of Law. The Vedic Expression that presents the structure of Law says, 'Know that by knowing which everything is known—by knowing which nothing any more remains to be known.'

Thoroughness of knowing lies in knowing

through direct experience. Experience identifies total awareness with the total creative potential of Natural Law, and this fully enlivens Natural Law on its own self-referral level and on all levels of its expression—intellectual, mental, sensory, behavioural, and environmental.

Knowledge gained through direct experience materializes intellectual understanding in practice. This is the way to gain mastery over management. The technique is: realize Law as the reality of one's Self, the reality of one's own intellect, the reality of one's own sensory perception.

It is beautifully fulfilling to see that the reality of these different levels of intelligence have sequentially* evolved into their own corresponding physiology.

Looking to the physiology as the expression of the intelligence of Law, we see that every individual is the embodiment of Law, the embodiment of the WHOLENESS of Law, the embodi-

---

* The mathematical perfection of this area of knowledge which deals with the origin and evolution of
Continued on page 288 ...

ment of the move of the WHOLENESS of Law—the embodiment of the reality of all possibilities.

Management is worthy of the name only if it utilizes the total potential of Law, and trains the individual to be the lively embodiment of Law, so that whatever work he is given to perform, he performs without violating Law—without violating his own nature—without violating his nature on the level of his Self, on the level of his intellect, on the level of his mind, on the level of his senses, on the level of his behaviour, and on the level of his whole environment, including the whole range of the distant horizons of the ever-expanding universe.

An individual so trained will be an embodiment of all Law and therefore will be incapable of violating any Law of Nature. A company of such individuals will enjoy the full support of Natural Law.

Everyone knows that violation of Law is a punishable offence. Violation of Natural Law causes problems and suffering in life and disorder in society, because Law is life, and therefore violation of Law is a violation of life—violation of Law is a crime against life.

The conclusion is that everyone must be trained to spontaneously use his creative potential—the creative potential of his Self, intellect, mind, senses, etc.

A company employs an individual who works for eight hours. If the company has not trained the individual to spontaneously use his full creativity, the output of work will be far, far below the potential possibility. The quality and the quantity will suffer, and what is more dangerous than even this is the violation of Natural Law; that means annoyance of the infinite organizing power of Natural Law, which will continue to shadow the whole fortune of the company, day after day, and create stress and strain on all levels of the company.

In this sense, every profession today is annoying to the evolutionary power of Natural Law because it is not following the natural, sequential evolution of Natural Law; it is violating the evolutionary power of Natural Law, as evidenced by the existing problems in the field of management.

Every management, whether of a family, a company, or a nation; any organization that is managing health, industry, rehabilitation, or defence; any government, big or small, must take notice of this proposed training in management in order to do justice to their position and authority to manage the destiny of their company. Maharishi University of Management has been established to help them all.

Maharishi's Master Management is TIMELY MANAGEMENT; it is that system of management which is spontaneously available to manage any situation, any responsibility, any problem, or manage anything at any time, under any situation or circumstance.

This quality of management will introduce automation in administration because it inspires the total managing intelligence of Nature—the infinite organizing power of Natural Law—to spontaneously uphold the managing intelligence of the individual manager; it is true for all times, progressive for all times, and fulfilling for all times.

Management through the managing intelligence

of Nature, because it supports the managing intelligence of the individual, is rightfully called TIMELY MANAGEMENT—management suitable for all times.

Timely Management TM
Maharishi's Master Management
is TIMELY MANAGEMENT
MMM is TM

Training in management at Maharishi University of Management develops expertise in TIMELY MANAGEMENT.

This means that whatever managerial skills or techniques or communication skills are needed at any time, in any place, or in any circumstance, the manager will have access to it in his awareness.

Training in 'TIMELY MANAGEMENT' means training in perfect management with the ability to manage anything successfully at any time. The manager will enjoy automation in administration by virtue of spontaneous involvement of the infinite organizing power of Natural Law in his every thought, speech, and action.

During his training at Maharishi University of Management, the individual creativity of the manager will rise to the performing level of Cosmic Creativity. He will develop intimacy with the Cosmic Creative Intelligence of Natural Law; he will learn to spontaneously manage time on the ground of the timelessness of Natural Law; he will learn to manage space from the field of the unboundedness of Natural Law; he will learn to manage his performance in any specific direction through the multi-directional performance of the holistic value of Natural Law.

Increasing mastery over Natural Law will give him the increasing ability to create:

- Problem-free management; a
- Harmonious, nourishing environment;
- Life in progress and fulfilment; and a
- Balanced, stable, and progressive economy.

Maharishi's Master Management is the post-industrial system of management, which has introduced the transcendental field—the holistic field of Natural Law—in all specific fields of management.

Being stationed at the common basis of all management, with the ability to engage the infinite organizing power of Natural Law, the graduate of Maharishi University of Management will be able to successfully manage the top level of administration in any field of life—including Politics; Economics; Education; Health; Law, Justice, and Rehabilitation; Agriculture; Industry; and Communication—and above all will learn how to engage the organizing power of Natural Law through mere desiring.

Within a few months he will realize that he can really handle the speedy progress of any undertaking, any company, or any government. The manager will realize that he has really gained sufficient confidence to accomplish anything. He will be the custodian of MAHARISHI'S MASTER MANAGEMENT, trained in TIMELY MANAGEMENT.

All the various fields of knowledge (and the organizing power of Natural Law) that are necessary for success at any time will spontaneously dawn in his awareness to support the timely need for successful management.

TIMELY MANAGEMENT is an expression that qualifies management and raises the quality of management to the level of its supreme efficiency and effectiveness; it raises the dignity of management to MAHARISHI'S MASTER MANAGEMENT.

Development of TIMELY MANAGEMENT is the goal of Maharishi University of Management, which offers the fruit of management to all—progressive success and fulfilment to the manager, to the managed, and to their relationship.

Maharishi's Master Management is available in the thirty-seven* textbooks of management through Natural Law—the Veda and Vedic Literature—which bring to light the laws that promote the mechanics of all possible systems of management in the ever-expanding universe.

Hundreds of textbooks on the thirty-seven areas of the total value of Natural Law and their divisions and subdivisions provide the knowledge of the absolute skill in management from all levels of the intelligence of the manager—his Self, his intellect, his mind, his senses, and his

---

* Refer to page 24.

behaviour, which influences his environment.

Perfection of training in management lies in utilizing all the techniques and tools that spontaneously develop the ability to perform simultaneously in all*directions from the fully lively field of pure Creative Intelligence. Refer to *Ṛicho Akshare* verse of Ṛk Veda (*Ṛk Veda, 1.164.39*), which presents Natural Law in the Transcendental Consciousness of everyone, and categorically states that Transcendental Consciousness is the home of all the Laws of Nature that govern the universe—the frequencies of Creative Intelligence, the Laws of Nature (mechanics of transformation), the self-referral performance of Natural Law responsible for the whole manifest universe—and indicates that it is possible for anyone to align his awareness with this total potential of Natural Law to gain perfection—balance in daily life.

Ṛicho Akshare is that verse of Ṛk Veda—that total expression of Natural Law—which has been shown to contain all the theories of all disciplines of modern science—Physics, Chemistry,

---

* Refer to pages 9 and 11.

etc. That is why training in management at Maharishi University of Management involves the study of this verse of Ṛk Veda, and through this involves all the theories of all disciplines of modern science in the field of management.

This is the reason why MBA's in management, graduating from Maharishi University of Management, will always have a successful career in any field of management that they choose to undertake.

Scientific*research has verified that alliance with Natural Law is gained by the mind through Maharishi's Transcendental Meditation. Transcendental Meditation is an essential feature of management training at Maharishi University of Management; that is why TIMELY MANAGEMENT (TM) is only available through Transcendental Meditation (TM).

Thus one can see that training in management at Maharishi University of Management is truly the phenomenon of the self-referral nature of perfect management, characterized by the quality of self-referral consciousness, which transcends

---

* Refer to pages 197–214.

the limitations of time, overriding any quality of time; it is not obstructed by any situation or circumstance; it is efficient, effective, and successful at all times, that is why it is true for all times—it is TIMELY MANAGEMENT—MAHARISHI'S MASTER MANAGEMENT.

Fundamental of Management
WHOLENESS

It is interesting and revealing that the infinite range of management has really only one fundamental, and that is WHOLENESS—Totality—all-comprehensive, eternal reality in its unmanifest, unbounded state of intelligence.

Fully awake, fully alert consciousness—singularity, WHOLENESS, aware of itself—spontaneously displays self-referral dynamism in terms of the sound of the Veda. This is how WHOLENESS, functioning within itself, generates impulses of WHOLENESS (structures of the Veda and Vedic Literature) which, continuing to evolve, express themselves as structures of Natural Law, evolving into material creation.

WHOLENESS appears as the Veda, Veda appears

Continued on page 87...

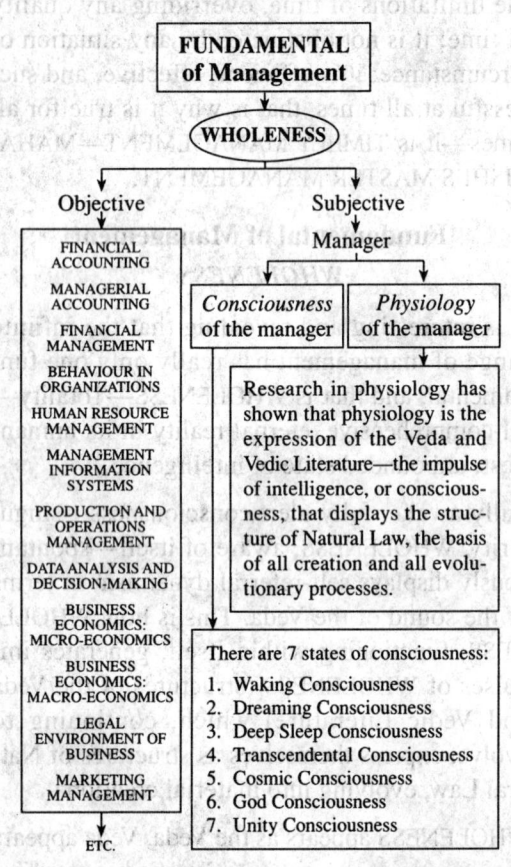

as the Laws of Nature, and this is the management of WHOLENESS—WHOLENESS managing itself through its own managing intelligence, the Laws of Nature that create, maintain, and evolve the entire ever-expanding universe within the structure of WHOLENESS.

It is interesting to see the internal mechanics of this management of WHOLENESS. The first thing to understand is that WHOLENESS has expressed itself in different impulses of Natural Law in terms of sound[*]—the Veda and Vedic Literature—the sound of the self-interacting dynamics of consciousness evolving into material creation—physiology and its environment.

Here is a picture of WHOLENESS demonstrated by the continuous sound अ ((A)[+], the first letter of Ṛk Veda), demonstrating infinity of silence—WHOLENESS of silence. Because infinity is just a sequentially organized infinite number of points, the relationship between infinity and point presents the WHOLENESS of silence in motion—silent WHOLENESS on the move—infinity of si-

---

[*] *Shruti*—that which is heard.

[+] Refer to page 101 (2nd footnote).

lence on the move—holistic value of silence on the move—holistic value of silence in terms of motion—WHOLENESS of silence in terms of WHOLENESS of motion, WHOLENESS of dynamism—two fullnesses emerging from one fullness. This is demonstrated by the first letter of Ṛk Veda and by the last letter of Ṛk Veda— from the first letter अ (A), WHOLENESS of silence, emerges the last letter इ (I), WHOLENESS of dynamism.

Here is a picture of two values of WHOLENESS—silence and dynamism—in one grand WHOLENESS of Natural Law.

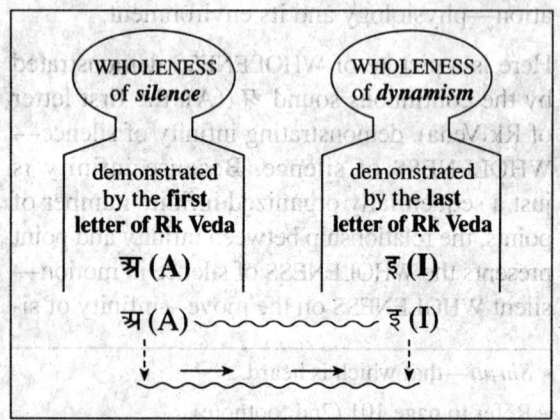

One WHOLENESS moving ⟶
to become another WHOLENESS—
WHOLENESS of silence moving between
infinity of silence, अ (A), and infinity of
dynamism, इ (I).

Ṛk Veda is the move of WHOLENESS to WHOLENESS. Ṛk Veda is the expression of the WHOLENESS of Natural Law in terms of silence and the WHOLENESS of Natural Law in terms of dynamism.

This is the fundamental principle of management: silence managing itself gets transformed into dynamism—silence by virtue of being fully awake within itself spontaneously finds itself in terms of dynamism.

In this picture we see the move of one WHOLENESS to another WHOLENESS. The whole Ṛk Veda—the whole field of Natural Law—sequentially emerging in specific structures of Natural Law (from अ (A) to इ (I)) demonstrates the move of WHOLENESS. One WHOLENESS moves to the other WHOLENESS; one WHOLENESS, इ (I), emerges from one WHOLENESS, अ (A).

This move of WHOLENESS displays the whole field of management on the level of the fundamental of management.

> Management is the phenomenon of WHOLENESS—from the wholeness of silence of the self-referral consciousness of the manager to the whole dynamic field of his activity of managing.

It is very interesting to observe the details of this march of WHOLENESS to WHOLENESS—WHOLENESS of silence to WHOLENESS of dynamism. One can locate the liveliness of precision and order in the unwavering march of WHOLENESS, from infinity of silence to infinity of dynamism; one sees the whole sequential development of the structures of Natural Law at every step of progression from अ (A) to* इ (I).

As it is the march of WHOLENESS, every step of progression in the whole length of Ṛk Veda,

---

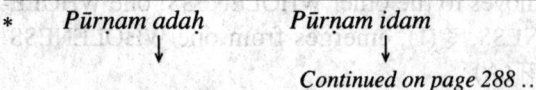

*   *Pūrṇam adaḥ*   *Pūrṇam idam*

Continued on page 288 ...

every word that sequentially follows every other word, every gap between words in every step that the holistic value of Natural Law takes during its move from infinity to infinity, is the step of WHOLENESS expressed in sequence by either a word or a gap.

The move of Natural Law is demonstrated by the sequentially organized steps of WHOLENESS perpetually maintained by every gap and every syllable, from the beginning to the end of Ṛk Veda.

It is this perpetual liveliness of the holistic move of Natural Law—from infinity of silence to infinity of dynamism—that spontaneously maintains the infinite, eternal organizing power at the basis of all creation and evolution.

The point to note here is that WHOLENESS is the fundamental of perfect management; WHOLENESS is the source of perfect management, WHOLENESS is the course of perfect management, and WHOLENESS is the goal of perfect management; that is why we say WHOLENESS is the fundamental of management. If management is to be perfect, the fundamental of management, WHOLENESS, should be lively in the awareness of the manager; then it is obvious that his managing capacity will be in alliance with the managing intelligence of Nature—the infinite organizing power of Natural Law.

As we have seen, perfection in management is the move of WHOLENESS within itself. As the wholeness of silence proceeds, in one sense the degree of silence sequentially becomes less and to the same extent the degree of dynamism increases. The net result is that at every step of evolution of Natural Law, as demonstrated by the sequentially evolving Rk Veda, there is a relationship between WHOLENESS of silence and WHOLENESS of dynamism. It is interesting to see that this coexistence of the opposite values of silence and dynamism creates what we know to be consciousness.

Consciousness is that element which is available in the coexistence of the opposite qualities of intelligence—one silence, one dynamism.

To enjoy the situation of the coexistence of silence and dynamism, it is interesting to observe that silence and dynamism, both characteristics of Natural Law, have to be on the extreme level of alertness, because if one is less alert than the other, then the more alert, more powerful, will overshadow the less alert, less powerful.

Therefore it is clear that consciousness is composed of two opposite qualities of Natural Law which provide a lively field of all possibilities to Maharishi's Master Management, the supreme ideal of management at any time, in any place, and under any situation and circumstance.

The manager trained in Maharishi's Master Management is never tossed about by situations and circumstances. Through the infinite organizing power of Natural Law he spontaneously maintains control over the whole range of his authority.

In order to understand the fundamental of management it is good to know that the laws that govern the wholesale market are different from those that govern the retail market; the laws that govern production are different from those that govern sales; the laws that govern the field of agriculture are different from those that govern industry; the laws that govern the life of the student are different from those that govern professional life; the laws that govern a city are different from those that govern a state, a nation, or the family of nations.

The areas that concern management are indeed numberless. It is not possible to have the knowledge of all the systems and all the laws that govern different fields of management, and without the knowledge of the laws that govern different aspects of the life of the individual, or national or international life, it is not possible to become a perfect manager. Therefore, it is very necessary to find a way so that even without the knowledge of all these innumerable laws that govern different areas of creation and evolution, the trained manager should be able to manage any field of management that he undertakes to

> manage from the basis of all the Laws of Nature, like a gardener who manages the whole tree by simply handling the root.
>
> To develop this quality of management it is necessary to gain the ability to handle the whole field of management from the fundamental of management—self-referral consciousness—WHOLENESS.

Supreme Management
Move of WHOLENESS

Management worth the name should be considered in terms of WHOLENESS.* The word management must be concerned with the move of WHOLENESS, and this move of WHOLENESS, throughout the range of any performance, is what renders management complete at every stage of progress—free from problems, and full of happiness and success at every step of progress. It is this quality of management that sub-

---

* Skill of management belongs to WHOLENESS; success belongs to WHOLENESS. Anyone who is
Continued on page 290 ...

stantiates the phrase 'automation in administration'.

The most important and most interesting area of knowledge about management is how WHOLENESS moves, and the most important and most interesting area of training of the manager is how he can imbibe in his awareness the mechanics of maintaining WHOLENESS while he is engaged in different areas of specific performance.

First we analyse the mechanics of 'WHOLENESS on the move'. We have already understood that WHOLENESS is self-referral consciousness, and that being self-referral consciousness it is aware of itself. This means that unbounded WHOLENESS is awake in the reality of the observer, the observed, and also the process of observation. Understanding this three-in-one structure of WHOLENESS is the foundation of WHOLENESS on the move within itself.

This three-in-one structure of WHOLENESS is

---

* Three-step move in one move of WHOLENESS. Those familiar with the Vedic Literature are aware of
Continued on page 293 ...

the reality of WHOLENESS moving within itself in three steps—WHOLENESS in action. This WHOLENESS in action being the nature of Unity, and Unity being the basis of diversity, makes it obvious that WHOLENESS on the move (Unity, moving within itself) is at the basis of the creation and orderly administration of the infinite diversity of the universe—this WHOLENESS on the move is the most fundamental mechanics of the whole creative process.

This is the level of Natural Law from where the infinitely diversified values of Natural Law emerge. The organizing power of Natural Law is eternally fully awake on this level of WHOLENESS. Therefore to maintain this level of WHOLENESS in the awareness of the manager is the goal of management training.

Now we will consider the principles and programmes whereby this supreme level of management can be enlivened in the consciousness of the manager. We have seen that self-referral consciousness is the fundamental of management, and this fundamental of management is fully lively and fully awake as the silent, dynamic, infinite organizing power of Natural Law, eternally displaying its nature in the move of WHOLENESS—the three-step move in one move of WHOLENESS—Saṁhitā of Ṛishi, Devatā, Chhandas.

This Saṁhitā of Ṛishi, Devatā, Chhandas, being self-referral consciousness, is the simplest state of human awareness. Bhagavad-Gītā, Yog-Shāstra, the treatise on the principle of Unity in diversity, lays out the performance from this simplest state of consciousness:

> सहजं कर्म कौन्तेय
> *Sahajaṁ karma Kaunteya*
> (Bhagavad-Gītā, 18.48)
>
> *Perform action from the natural state of consciousness—perform action from that level of consciousness where consciousness is in its simplest state.*

Here is the formula for perfect management: management should be handled from the simplest state of consciousness.

Ideal management training requires that during training the manager should stabilize the habit of functioning from the simplest state of consciousness, which we have understood to be WHOLE-

NESS—fully comprehensive, all-encompassing level of intelligence—unbounded, transcendental level of consciousness—unmanifest, unqualified, pure totality of intelligence, which is expressed by the Vedic Term, Saṁhitā of Ṛishi, Devatā, Chhandas, which by nature is eternally on the move within itself.

Saṁhitā is eternally*Saṁhitā (unified WHOLENESS, self-awareness), and it is eternally Ṛishi, Devatā, Chhandas; and Ṛishi, Devatā, Chhandas are eternally⁺three qualities of Saṁhitā. This emergence of Ṛishi, Devatā, Chhandas from Saṁhitā, and submergence of Ṛishi, Devatā,

---

* This beautiful level of management is described by the Yog-Sūtra:

स्वरूपेऽवस्थानम्
Swarūpe avasthānam (Yog-Sūtra, 1.3)
The observer is established in himself.

⁺ This beautiful level of management is described by the Yog-Sūtra:

वृत्तिसारूप्यमितरत्र
Vṛitti sārūpyam itaḥ atra (Yog-Sūtra, 1.4)
Tendencies (of the observer) *emerge from here* (self-referral state) *and remain here* (within the self-referral state).

Chhandas into Saṁhitā continues with infinite frequency—the move* of WHOLENESS within itself with infinite frequency. This is the infinite dynamism in silence, which is the infinite creative intelligence at the basis of all creation and evolution.

What is most valuable here, in the context of management training, is that this level of reality is the simplest state of human consciousness, which can be accessed by anyone through my Transcendental Meditation; and this simplest state of consciousness can be stabilized by everyone in his daily life through the advanced practices of Transcendental Meditation, including Yogic Flying.

In the chapter on Transcendental Meditation and Yogic Flying all these mechanics have been explained. (Refer to pages 174–189.)

It is interesting to see that the progressive

---

* The theories of the pulsating universe and wave function of the universe (Quantum Cosmology) offer their profound achievement in this direction.

structure of the Constitution of Natural Law in Ṛk Veda expresses WHOLENESS at every step of progression.

WHOLENESS is expressed through the first letter of Ṛk Veda: अ (A);[+]

WHOLENESS is expressed through the first syllable of Ṛk Veda: अक् (Ak);

WHOLENESS is expressed through the first word of Ṛk Veda: अग्निम् *Agnim*;

WHOLENESS is expressed through the first *Richā* (verse) of Ṛk Veda:

अग्निमीळे पुरोहितं
यज्ञस्य देवमृत्विजम्
होतारं रत्नधातमम्

Agnimīle purohitaṁ
yagyasya devam ṛitvijam
hotāraṁ ratna dhātamam

---

[*] These different expressions are the quantified values of the evolving structure of knowledge in Ṛk Veda.

[+] The first letter of Ṛk Veda is अ (A). It stands to represent the total field of knowledge, the total field

Continued on page 294 ...

WHOLENESS is expressed through the first* *Sūkta* (collection of 9 *Richā*) of Ṛk Veda;

WHOLENESS is expressed through the first* *Maṇḍala* of Ṛk Veda (192 *Sūkta* arranged in a *Maṇḍala*—indestructible continuum):

WHOLENESS is expressed through the ten *Maṇḍals* of Ṛk Veda:

WHOLENESS is expressed through the six⁺ Veda: Sāma Veda, Yajur-Veda, Atharva

---

* Refer to page 101 (1st footnote).

⁺ Veda, Vedāṅga, Upāṅga, Āyur-Veda, Brāhmaṇa, and Prātishākhya are the six areas of the Vedic Literature.

Continued on page 303 …

Veda, Sthāpatya Veda, Dhanur-Veda, and Gandharva Veda;

WHOLENESS is expressed through the six Vedānga: Shikshā, Kalp, Vyākaraṇ, Nirukt, Chhand, Jyotish;

WHOLENESS is expressed through the six Upānga*: Nyāya, Vaisheshik, Sāṁkhya, Yoga, Karma Mīmāṁsā, Vedānt;

WHOLENESS is expressed through the six Saṁhitā of Āyur-Veda: Charak, Sushrut, Vāgbhatt, Bhāva-Prakāsh, Shārngadhar, Mādhav Nidān;

WHOLENESS is expressed through the six Brāh*maṇa[+]: Smṛiti, Purāṇ, Itihās, Brāhmaṇa, Āraṇyak, Upanishad;

WHOLENESS is expressed through the six Pratishākhyas*: Ṛk Veda Prātishākhya,

---

* Refer to page 102 (2nd footnote).

[+] Veda is knowledge which is composed of Mantra and Brāhmaṇa. Mantra is the expression of Law,
Continued on page 305 ...

> Shukl-Yajur-Veda Prātishākhya, Krishṇ-Yajur-Veda Prātishākhya (*Taittirīya*), Sāma Veda Prātishākhya (*Pushpa Sūtram*), Atharva Veda Prātishākhya, Atharva Veda Prātishākhya (*Chaturadhyāyi*).

The sequential development of knowledge available in the structure of Ṛk Veda presents the most natural, perfect theme of evolution of WHOLENESS. This evolving structure of WHOLENESS—Natural Law, the frequencies of Veda, *Shruti*—continues to move, propelled by the inital momentum of its self-referral dynamics, creating the fabrics of material creation in perfect order.

Because this move of WHOLENESS is unavailable in modern management training, the manager fails to manage himself, fails to successfully manage his company, and fails to have an enriching influence on his environment. That is why the whole field of management is a failure for the health and happiness of the manager, for the well-being and progress of the company, and for its enriching, nourishing effect in the environment.

The whole field of management is a field of stress and strain. It is only polluting to life because it has no basis.

The manager is the father of the company in the same way as the President is the father of the country. He is responsible to nourish everyone and help everyone to evolve to greater levels of success, not only in the life of the company, but in the life of every individual involved in the company. He is expected to be the wisest in the company. His thinking and planning should make the company grow, and this growth should be in the direction of the unrestricted evolution of Natural Law in the life of the company, in the company as a whole, and in everyone individually. This is his pious concern for all those who serve him.

The manager should be able to enlighten everyone in his company. He should be like a father, to nourish; a teacher, to enlighten; and a guiding light, to lead everyone on the path to ultimate fulfilment.

Education and training in management does not give enough importance to developing the consciousness, or intelligence, of the manager.

Maharishi University of Management, providing the complete theory and practical programmes to develop the full creative genius of every student, develops in him perfection as far as perfection is possible.

In the problem-ridden environment of today's world of management, this knowledge of management through Natural Law is gaining popularity. The problems of the world, rooted in the undeveloped intelligence of the manager, will now simply disappear.

Broad Comprehension and Ability to Focus Sharply

Training in management should have the elements of knowledge that will create and maintain the whole range of management, holistic and specific, in the simplest state of awareness of the manager, so that whatever specific value he manages, his process of management is always spontaneously upheld by the holistic value of Cosmic Management—the infinite organizing power of Natural Law.

Development of this ability to spontaneously harness the infinite organizing power of the administrative intelligence of the universe will ensure that no aspect of management ever has a chance to deviate from the royal road of evolution, the royal road of success, the royal road of fulfilment, because the supreme intelligence—Cosmic Intelligence of the universe—spontaneously manages the evolution of everything and everyone, while promoting the evolution of the universe as a whole.

The actual training of top level management requires the development of the HABIT to spontaneously maintain the awareness of the total field of management while focusing on any one specific area of management.

Training in management requires the development of the ability to focus on one specific area of any project without losing the broad comprehension of the entire field of the project.

The most successful procedure for the development of this quality in the manager is regular practice of Transcendental Meditation, which has demonstrated the growth of field[*] independence—the spontaneous ability to maintain broad comprehension while focusing sharply on any one area.

The Science and Art of Management
Purity of Life Is the Basis of Success

The Vedic theme of management through Natural Law is based on the unifying power of Natural Law—

निस्त्रैगुरायो भवार्जुन
Nistrai-guṇyo bhav-Arjuna—
(Bhagavad-Gītā, 2.45)

come to the field of Unity, or bring your awareness to Transcendental Consciousness, and there is the Unified Field of Natural Law, the concentrated field of intelligence—the source of all

---

[*] Scientific[+] research has shown that through regular practice of the Transcendental Meditation and TM-
Continued on page 305 ...

[+] Refer to the scientific journal *Perceptual and Motor Skills*, 39 (1974): 1031–1034.

evolutionary trends of life from where the whole creation, the ever-expanding universe, is spontaneously materialized.

This is the field of intelligence from where the management of the ever-evolving, ever-expanding universe is spontaneously conducted; therefore training in management should be to bring the manager's awareness to this level of intelligence, and then training in management will have a supreme quality. For this, the commonly known proverb in India is:

क्रियासिद्धिः सत्त्वे भवति महतां नोपकरणे
*Kriyā siddhiḥ sattwe bhavati
mahatāṁ nopakaraṇe
The success of 'great men' comes from
their self-referral, unbounded field of intelligence—coherent consciousness (Sattwa)—and basically not from the means
of operation.*

The reality is that the means gather around *Sāttwik* intelligence—Natural Law favours *Sāttwik* consciousness—and whatever is required, comes.

The point to note here is that in this field of unbounded consciousness—in Unity Consciousness, which is the simplest state of human consciousness—there is nothing else other than self-referral consciousness itself, so the achievement of managing the enormous, unbounded field of the universe from this level is solely dependent on this level of Transcendental Consciousness, because there is nothing else; that is why the second part of the above quotation negates the requirement of any other means for absolute success in management.

The idea is that when the awareness of the manager is open to this field of the concentrated creative intelligence of Natural Law, then the thought of achieving anything spontaneously motivates all the Laws of Nature required to materialize the desire. But if the manager is busy searching for the means of 'hitting the target', then his active mind does not have the support of the transcendental, total potential of the organizing power of Natural Law; then his approach to achievement will certainly be through situations and circumstances in his environment, which will make him prone to stress, strain, and struggle to achieve the target.

This makes it clear why the system of modern management is subject to stress, strain, and struggle for its achievement, which spreads the quality of stress and strain and promotes all that stress and strain can offer to society.

The system of administration through Natural Law, Maharishi's Master Management, comes as a solution to all problems in the world—problems of politics, economics, health, education—and all areas of national and international life in every country.

The modern system of management does not train managers in the science and art of gaining alliance with the infinite organizing power of Natural Law—the managing intelligence of Nature—because while the manager is engaged in gaining the knowledge of different areas of management, the system of management itself deprives him of his own self-referral consciousness and engages him in the field of variety, segregating his functioning intelligence from its infinite creative potential. He becomes dependent on the limited creative potential of isolated systems of management and falls a prey to stress and strain.

The point to note here is that modern training in management is not based on the principle and practical application of the transcendental value of the holistic value of Natural Law. The sole focus of modern management training is in the importance of gathering the means of management.

The field of management is so vast and varied that unless the managing intelligence of the manager is embedded in the infinite organizing power of Natural Law—the managing intelligence of Nature—it will always be under stress and strain.

The Goal of Maharishi University of Management

Maharishi University of Management has been established with the goal of eliminating problems in the world.

Problems are the products of bad management, mismanagement, incomplete management.

There is something of a fundamental nature

missing in leading institutions of management, which is causing stress in the managers and their systems of managing. There is a global*cry for help evidenced by articles in the world press and in leading management journals, which calls for a more complete and more perfect system of management.

The secret of successful management is lively within the word 'University':

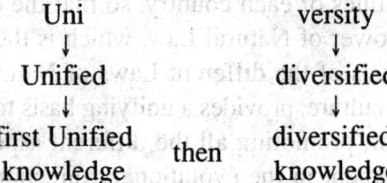

Maharishi University of Management has been established to be the guiding light for all institutes of management in the world.

In any big or small machine the looseness of one little screw makes the whole machine rattle. We can imagine what can
----

* Refer to pages 236–248.

> happen when the very design of the machine lacks completeness!

The plan is that Maharishi University of Management will inspire the establishment of Institutes of Management in every major country of the world in order to offer its ideal system of management in harmony with the precious cultural values of each country, so that the organizing power of Natural Law, which is the common basis of the different Laws of Nature that uphold culture, provides a unifying basis to management, promoting all the different aspects of management in the evolutionary direction—the direction of Natural Law.

This will be a way to save the dignity of every nation in the competitive international markets. In every nation it is very important that the

---

* *USA TODAY*, 9 November 1993, in its article 'Harvard plans to retool MBA curriculum' states:

Harvard business school is proposing to revamp its curriculum for a Master of Business
Continued on page 308 …

people of every generation remain connected to their cultural*values. Life according to one's culture means life spontaneously in the evolutionary direction of Natural Law.

Importance of Culture
Spontaneous Application of Natural Law to Management

Maharishi University of Management is starting to create brilliant managers in the world who will introduce perfect management—ideal management — invincible management — and will achieve automation in administration under their leadership. This is because Maharishi University of Management utilizes Natural Law to make management perfect.

The consideration of culture becomes very important in any country if management is to be raised to perfection, because culture has its basis in Natural Law, and the growth of life is nourished by the spontaneous application of

---

* *India Business Intelligence* (newsletter of the *FINANCIAL TIMES*), 2 November 1994, in its article
Continued on page 308 ...

Natural Law in the habits of the people—in the trends and tendencies of the nation.

For management to be perfect and really rewarding for all concerned, it is very important that foreign ideologies do not dominate the life of the manager and the system of management that connects him with his field of responsibility. Therefore in the training of managers the consideration of cultural values must be taken into account.

One thing is very fulfilling in the teaching of management at Maharishi University of Management and this is that both values of Natural Law, holistic and specific, are combined to make management perfect.

The holistic value of Natural Law is Cosmic Creative Intelligence, which administers the infinite diversity of the universe holistically, and maintains the integration between innumerable specific administrative aspects of intelligence that can be specified in terms of the intelligence of the administration of galaxies, solar systems, and our planet earth. These different levels of administration have different specific qualities, but permeating all of them is one holistic quality of intelligence—one holistic quality of administration.

The holistic value of Natural Law handles the holistic value of culture—universal culture—whereas specific values of different Laws of Nature are concerned with the specific culture of an individual country or the specific area of a country; these are the Laws of Nature that give rise to the specific geographic and climatic conditions, accents of speech, languages, and trends of society on all levels of life—spiritual, social, and material.

Management in every country should fundamentally be based on the cultural values of the country, and on this ground of the spontaneous ability to maintain cultural values, the use of modern tools and techniques of communication will be sufficient to compete and come out successful in the local, national, and international competitive markets.

Management in every country will be

> more rewarding if it is in the local language of the people, because communication is easier, smoother, and more thorough in one's mother tongue.
>
> The trained, skilled manager should use the mother tongue of the people who are being managed by him, so that there is not a culture gap or language gap to break communication.
>
> Maharishi University of Management has a programme to train managers in each country in their own local language. This will make the procedure of managing the local people more effective, easy, and thorough.

Problems of lack of resources, and the rise of stress and strain, which are widely common in the field of management, do not belong to the management of Natural Law. The reason is that Natural Law is infinitely resourceful and creative and therefore capable of operating through the 'PRINCIPLE OF LEAST ACTION'.

Parental Role of Management

- The nature of life is to grow.

- Creative Intelligence is at the basis of growth.

- Whenever Creative Intelligence lacks the opportunity to express itself fully, growth is obstructed, and life, whose nature is to grow, begins to suffer.

- The routine of life keeps the awareness within boundaries, and boundaries made rigid day by day offer increasing resistance to the free flow of Creative Intelligence.

- Life has ever been lived through boundaries—through the same channels of perception, thinking, and action. That is why there has been no opportunity for the free and FULL expression of Creative Intelligence in the daily routine of life.

- The increasing rigidity of boundaries caused by the daily routine of life is responsible for the age-old experience of mankind that life is a struggle. The routine nature of the work required by this technological age has merely intensified the problem.

- Routine work produces rigidity of boundaries and this restricts opportunity for the full expression of Creative Intelligence. However, routine work offers disciplined activity which adds efficiency to progress. Thus we find that even though routine work is damaging to the nature of life, it is at the same time helpful for progress in the outside world.

- It is not necessary to forgo either life for progress or progress for life. It is not necessary to forgo routine work because it is possible now to neutralize its harmful, narrowing effects.

- Here, in the lack of opportunity for the full expression of Creative Intelligence, is the seed of discontent in man. It sprouts in frustration at work and grows into general dissatisfaction, overshadowing even the soothing love of family and friends.

- Because the seed of discontent is LACK (of opportunity for the full expression of Creative Intelligence) and because lack is just the absence of something, there is nothing one can lay one's hands on. That is why the basic cause of discontent remains hidden, unrecognized.

One remains the victim of what this lack produces—discontent, frustration, negativity, and all the problems they engender.

- **My Vedic Science, with its practical aspect, Transcendental Meditation, provides an opportunity for the FULL expression of Creative Intelligence. The daily opportunity for the individual's awareness to go beyond boundaries neutralizes the rigidity caused by the boundaries of the daily routine.**

- My Vedic Science has demonstrated the possibility of eliminating the age-old problems of mankind in this generation.

- Modern man does not have to continue to live with the old experience of struggle and suffering.

It may be interesting for thinkers and leaders of society today to review an expansion of the philosophy outlined above, along with a consideration of recent findings of scientific research on Transcendental Meditation, developed in terms of Physiology and Quantum Physics. (Refer to pages 197–218.)

It may be seen that the principles upholding the practical application of my Vedic Science have their basis in the universal Laws of Nature and therefore are readily adaptable to all practical dimensions of life.

My Vedic Science has been amply validated by both scientific[*] research and subjective[+] experience as a simple, natural, and efficient procedure for developing the full creative potential of the individual, and there is no reason why everyone should not take immediate advantage of it to quickly and directly improve the quality of his life and the success of his career.

---

[*] Refer to pages 197–203.

[+] Refer to Maharishi Vedic University Press publication *Prachetanā—Fully Awakened Consciousness*, *Continued on page 312 ...*

Natural Law, Cosmic Manager of the Universe, Invincible Source of Order and Harmony Discovered in the Human Physiology

With the knowledge and understanding of my Vedic Science, Tony Nader, M.D., Ph.D., has discovered* the relationship between consciousness and physiology, by correlating all the thirty-seven aspects of the physiology with the thirty-seven values of consciousness, or intelligence.

The self-referral state of human consciousness, which is easily accessible to everyone through my Transcendental Meditation, has been identified as the self-sufficient source of pure knowledge and its infinite organizing power—the home✢ of all the Laws of Nature, the holistic structure of all the Laws of Nature displayed in

---

* Refer to Maharishi Vedic University Press publication, *Human Physiology—Expression of Veda and the Vedic Literature*.

✢ यस्मिन् देवा अधि विश्वे निषेदुः
 Yasmin Devā adhi vishwe nisheduh
   (Rk Veda, 1.164.39)

Continued on page 312 ...

Ṛk Veda, the Constitution of the Universe, and its structuring dynamics, differentiated structures of all the Laws of Nature available in the Vedic Literature.

It is fulfilling to know that the structure of the holistic value of Natural Law is Ṛk Veda Saṁhitā, and the structuring dynamics of Ṛk Veda Saṁhitā are the thirty-six values of the Vedic Literature.

The holistic structure of Natural Law is Ṛk Veda, and the differentiated structures of the Laws of Nature are available in the Vedic Literature as the *Sūtra*, or verses, of the Vedic Literature.

This unified holistic structure of Natural Law and these diversified differentiated structures of the Laws of Nature have now been discovered as the fundamental basis and essential ingredient of the human physiology.

This is the time after thousands of years of ignorance of the concrete structures and functions of Natural Law that they are now available for intelligent use by individu*als, by na-

---

* Transcendental Meditation and the TM-Sidhi Programme. (Refer to pages 174–189.)

tions*, and by the whole family⁺ of nations to achieve perfection on every level of life.

It will be interesting to now consider the **thirty-seven values of the Constitution of the Universe**—the unified value of Natural Law in Ṛk Veda and the diversified values of the Laws of Nature in the Vedic Literature—the structuring intelligence at the basis of the thirty-seven areas of the human physiology.

This integrated understanding that Veda is at the basis of the physiology is new; it has two different terminologies: the terminology of the objective field of modern physiology, and the Vedic approach of the subjective field of intelligence.

This knowledge can easily be understood in every

---

* Maintaining 'A Group for A Government'—a group of Yogic Flyers for a government—to create the *Maharishi Effect* in national consciousness (refer to page 190), and a group of Yogic Flyers, an auxiliary defence force—a PREVENTION WING for the military—to prevent the birth of an enemy.

⁺ Maintaining a group of 7,000 in each continent to create the *Global Maharishi Effect* for invincibility to every nation, securing invincible defence for the whole world. (Refer to page 193.)

country by medical doctors who have studied modern medicine and are aware that the structure and function of the physiology can be classified into thirty-seven areas. However, this knowledge can also easily be grasped by every individual because it is the reality at the basis of everyone's physiology.

It is interesting to see the correspondence between these modern and ancient terminologies with reference to the physiology and its internal intelligence, making it clear that the thirty-seven areas of the human physiology are essentially the expressions of the thirty-seven areas of intelligence, or consciousness, as available in the Veda and Vedic Literature.

The discovery of the Veda and Vedic Literature at the basis of the human physiology presents the cognition of the structure and function of Natural Law and, through the application of this knowledge, provides a highway to perfection for any individual and any nation.

Let us have the vision of the two expressions of Natural Law—one on the level of sound (the field of speech), and one on the level of form (the level of the physiology—the expression of the Laws of Nature).

The knowledge, at a glance, contained in the chart on pages 130–131, reveals that the structure of Natural Law in terms of structures of sound (the field of speech), as available in the Vedic Literature, is expressed in material form (the level of physiology—the expression of the Laws of Nature) in the human physiology.

These two structures of Natural Law—one on the level of intelligence in the form of sound (Veda), and the other in the form of matter (physiology)—are the cognitions of the structures of Natural Law on concrete levels of perception.

This is the reliable structure of total knowledge that my Vedic Science and Technology provides, which offers all possibilities to everyone.

The thirty-seven clusters of Natural Law and their divisions at the basis of all the processes of creation and evolution are available to us in the Veda and Vedic Literature, and are expressed in the structure and function of the human physiology.

It is necessary that all these values of Natural Law always remain fully awake within the physiology of everyone so that all thought, speech, and action can always be according to Natural Law, so that no one violates Natural Law and no one creates the ground for suffering.

Innumerable books can be written to glorify this inner intelligence of every individual, and when we look to the world literature from the platform of religion we find that the great enlightened knowers of reality, the sages and seers and the prophets and incarnations of God, have all sung the glory of God in man, and all have required that this inner intelligence should be fully enlivened for everyone to live the grace of God.

In the cherished textbooks of every religion one finds the knowledge to enliven this inner intelligence and the requirement of life to maintain the integrated relationship between mind and body.

The great power of prayers, advocated in the honoured texts of every religion, are just to provide an opportunity to every individual to align his awareness with the invincible, almighty, merciful, evolutionary power of Natural Law—

the Will of God—and live daily life on the ground of invincibility—the invincible armour of God's Will—the invincible protection and support of the infinite organizing power of Natural Law.

Since time immemorial, the Veda and Vedic Literature have been held to be the expression of the total knowledge of Natural Law—the expression of the inner intelligence in creation—the expression of the inner intelligence of every aspect of the physiology.

This knowledge has bridged the gap between mind and body, between consciousness and physiology, and between the individual, the environment, and the universe. It has provided the practicality of living a balanced life in accordance with the evolutionary theme of Natural Law—ranging from point to infinity.

The discovery of the one-to-one relationship between the structure and function of the Veda and Vedic Literature and the structure and function of the human physiology has established beyond a doubt that human physiology is the expression of Natural Law from the point of view of mod-

Continued on page 169 ...

Constitution of the Universe
Ṛk Veda and Vedic Literature
The Structuring Dynamics of Natural Law Present within the Self of Everyone

Ātmā, the source of Veda, fully awake in its potentiality is Totality—***Brahm***. *Ātmā* is lively in its full potential when its self-interacting dynamics, the thirty-seven values of the Vedic Literature, together give rise to the structure of the Veda (pure knowledge)—the Laws of Nature,

Constitution of the Universe
Ṛk Veda and Vedic Literature

Expressed in the Structure and Function
of the Physiology of Everyone

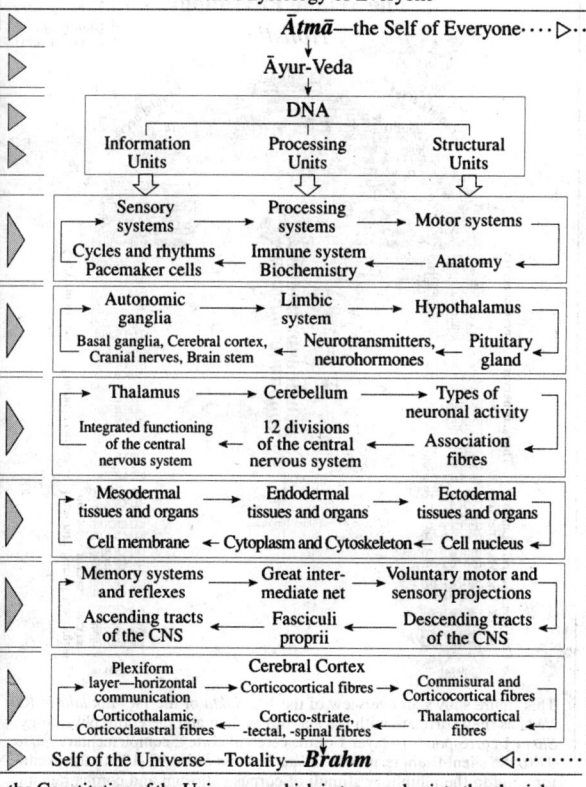

the Constitution of the Universe—which in turn evolve into the physiology and the material creation (*Vishwa*) while ever remaining within the field of *Ātmā*. This *Ātmā*—*Ātmā* with the total memory of Veda and *Vishwa* within it—is *Brahm*, the Totality—**Ayam Ātmā Brahm.**

ṚK VEDA
The Whole Physiology
Holistic

Vedic Term
Physiological Term
Quality of Consciousness

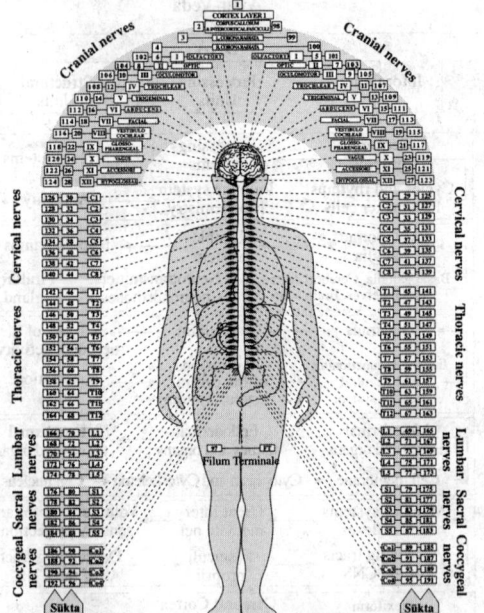

This figure shows an overview of the 192 *Sūkta* of the 1st *Maṇḍala* of Ṛk Veda as they correlate with the nervous system and the entire physiology: *Sūkta* 1 corresponds to layer 1 of the cerebral cortex; complementary *Sūkta* 97 to the silent filum terminale; *Sūkta* 2–4 and *Sūkta* 98–100 to the excitatory and to the inhibitory stimuli of corpus callosum and corona radiata; *Sūkta* 5–28 and 101–124 to the excitatory and inhibitory stimuli of the 24 cranial nerves; *Sūkta* 29–96 and 125–192 to the excitatory and inhibitory stimuli of the spinal nerves.

Vedic Term
Physiological Term
Quality of Consciousness

SĀMA VEDA
Sensory Systems
Flowing Wakefulness

133

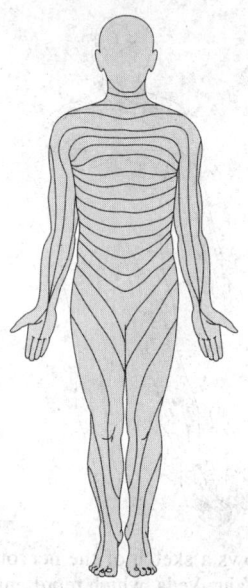

This figure shows the dermatomes related to the spinal sensory nerves as an illustration of Sāma Veda, which represents the totality of the Ṛishi value (knower, wakefulness)—all sensory aspects in the five sensory modalities.

There are 1,000 *Shākhās* or branches of Sāma Veda. They correspond in the human body to 1,000 'doorways' of perception.

YAJUR-VEDA
Processing Systems
Dynamic, Creative

] Vedic Term
] Physiological Term
] Quality of Consciousness

134

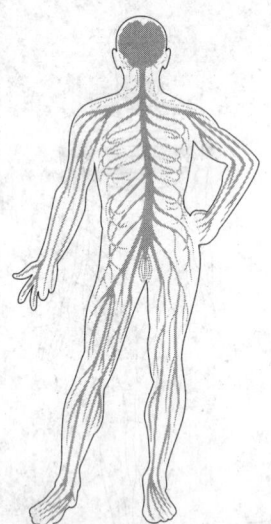

This figure shows a sketch of the nervous system as an illustration of Yajur-Veda, which represents the totality of Devatā value (dynamism): processing, integrating, interpreting, and creating.

There are 2 categories of Yajur-Veda that together comprise 21 divisions. One of these 21 divisions contains 40 chapters. The central nervous system is anatomically and embryologically divided into 40 divisions corresponding to the 40 chapters in Yajur-Veda.

Vedic Term — **ATHARVA VEDA** 135
Physiological Term — **Motor Systems**
Quality of Consciousness — *Reverberating WHOLENESS*

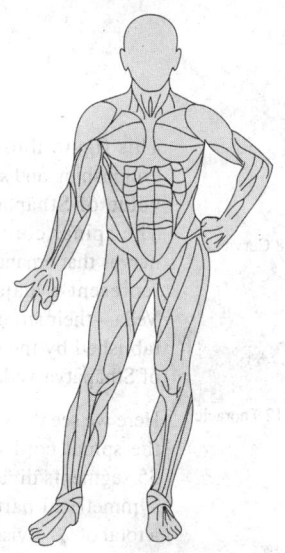

This figure shows some of the muscle groups of the body as an illustration of Atharva Veda, representing Saṁhitā (unified value) with a predominance of Chhandas value (covering, hiding, expanding, and moving all over the body).

In Atharva Veda there are 9 *Shākhās* or branches. The musculo-skeletal system is made of 9 divisions: 1. Head, 2. Neck, 3. Upper limbs, 4. Thorax, 5. Back, 6. Abdomen, 7. Pelvis, 8. Perineum, 9. Lower limbs.

136 STHĀPATYA VEDA
Anatomy
Established in Itself

] Vedic Term
] Physiological Term
] Quality of Consciousness

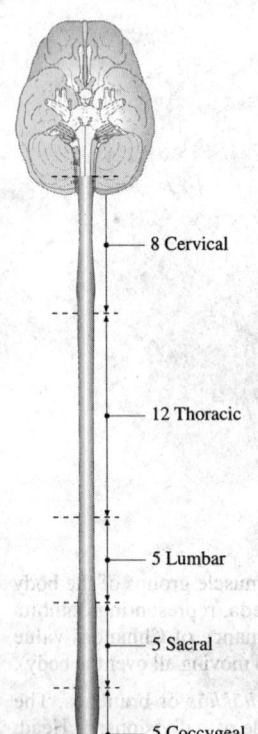

- 8 Cervical
- 12 Thoracic
- 5 Lumbar
- 5 Sacral
- 5 Coccygeal

This figure illustrates the establishing and structuring value of Sthāpatya Veda. The spinal cord with the nerves that emanate from it represent a major part of Veda—their structure is established by the principles of Sthāpatya Veda.

Here we see the structure of the spinal cord which has 35 segments divided into 2 symmetrical parts making a total of 70 divisions. They correspond to the 70 chapters of Sthāpatya Veda.

Vedic Term — **DHANUR-VEDA**
Physiological Term — **Immune System, Biochemistry**
Quality of Consciousness — ***Invincible and Progressive***

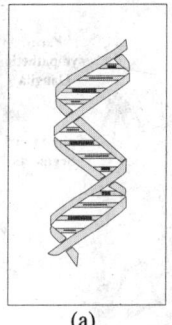

(a)

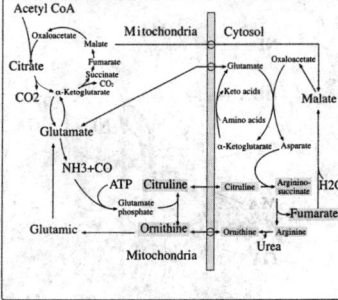

(b)

This figure shows three pictures illustrating Dhanur-Veda on three different levels. The first one (a) shows the DNA, which in its self-referral silence and dynamism is projected into the entire human physiology (the 'Self' of DNA—*Ātmā*—is projected into the entire diversity of the body—*Brahm*). The second (b) shows biochemical reactions which project one state into another. The arrows between molecules represent the value of transformation similar to the theme of bow and arrow in Dhanur-Veda. The third (c) shows the vertebral column. Each vertebra is divided into 4 parts. They correspond to the 4 chapters of Dhanur-Veda. There are 33 vertebrae. Every chapter in Dhanur-Veda contains a number of *Sūtra* which is, in every case, a multiple of 33, reflecting exactly the structure and function of the vertebral column.

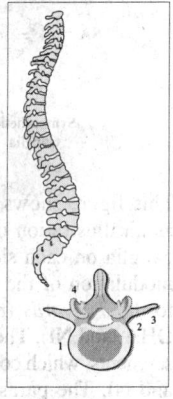

(c)

GANDHARVA VEDA

Cycles and Rhythms, Pacemaker Cells
Integrating and Harmonizing

> Vedic Term
> Physiological Term
> Quality of Consciousness

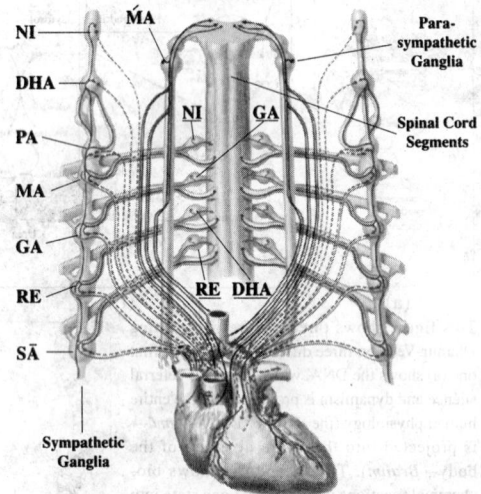

This figure shows the heart and its neuronal innervation as an illustration of Gandharva Veda. Seven sympathetic ganglia on each side of the spinal cord participate in the modulation of the rhythms of the heart. They correspond to the 7 *Swaras* (musical notes) (SĀ, RE, GA, MA, PA, DHA, and NI). These impulses are connected to 4 thoracic segments, which correspond to the flat notes RE, GA, DHA, and NI. The parasympathetic (vagal) innervation corresponds to the sharp note ḾA.

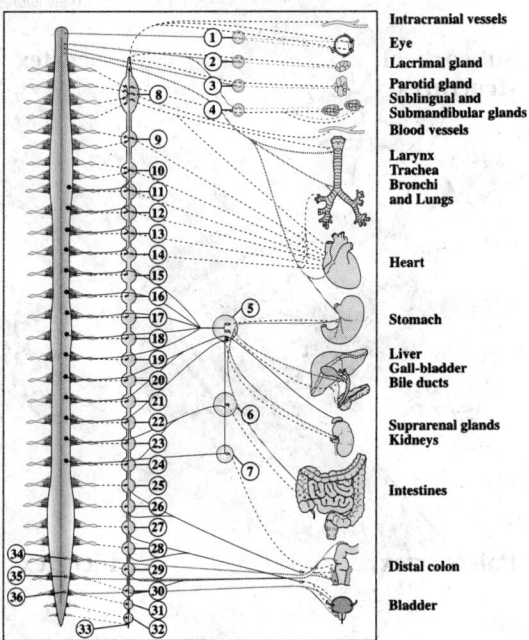

SHIKSHĀ
Autonomic Ganglia
(36 ganglia)
Expression

Vedic Term — Physiological Term — Quality of Consciousness

Labels: Intracranial vessels; Eye; Lacrimal gland; Parotid gland; Sublingual and Submandibular glands; Blood vessels; Larynx, Trachea, Bronchi and Lungs; Heart; Stomach; Liver, Gall-bladder, Bile ducts; Suprarenal glands, Kidneys; Intestines; Distal colon; Bladder

This figure shows 36 autonomic ganglia with some of the tissues and organs to which they connect. They correspond to the 36 books of Shikshā.

140   KALP

Limbic System
(4 divisions with 19, 8, 1,
and 12 divisions respectively)

Transformation

Vedic Term

Physiological Term

Quality of Consciousness

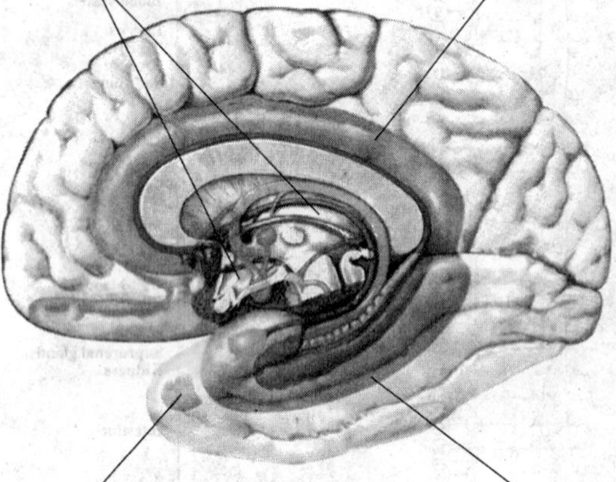

Subcortical structures

Mesocortex

Paleocortex

Archicortex

This figure shows the limbic system with its 4 parts and their divisions. They correspond to the 4 parts and sub-divisions of Kalp.

Vedic Term	**VYĀKARAṆ**	141

Hypothalamus
(8 regions with 4 nuclei each)

Expansion

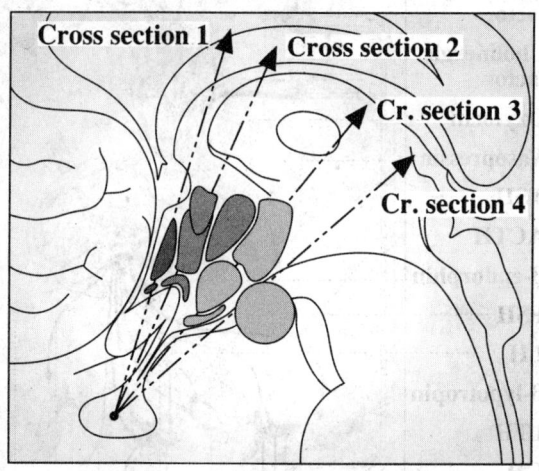

This figure shows the 4 levels of the cross-section of the cerebral cortex, delineating 8 areas of the hypothalamus: anterior, posterior, middle, and lateral, each right and left, with their respective 4 nuclei on either side, adding up to 32 nuclei, which correspond to the 8 chapters of 4 sections each, totalling 32 divisions of Vyākaraṇ.

142

NIRUKT
Pituitary Gland
(13 factors)
Self-Referral

] *Vedic Term*
] *Physiological Term*
] *Quality of Consciousness*

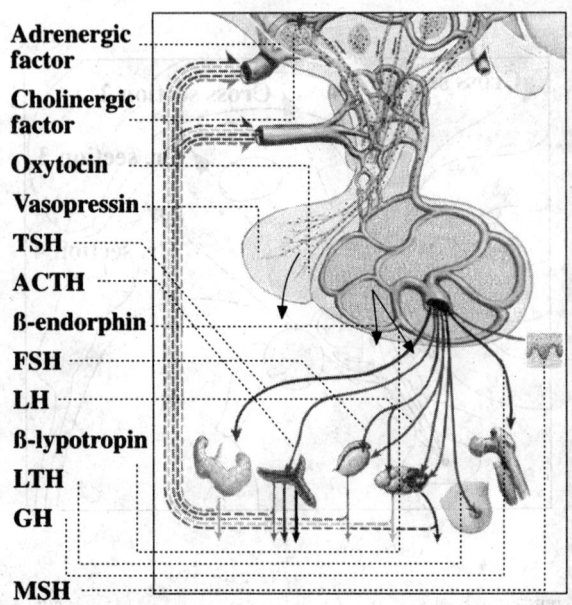

- Adrenergic factor
- Cholinergic factor
- Oxytocin
- Vasopressin
- TSH
- ACTH
- ß-endorphin
- FSH
- LH
- ß-lypotropin
- LTH
- GH
- MSH

This figure shows the hypothalamus as it activates the autonomic nervous system and the pituitary gland. The 13 factors involved in the response to the hypothalamus correspond to the 13 chapters of Nirukt.

		143
Vedic Term	**CHHAND**	
Physiological Term	**Neurohormones, Neurotransmitters, and their receptors acting on the end-organs classified into 8 organ systems**	
Quality of Consciousness	*Measuring and Quantifying*	

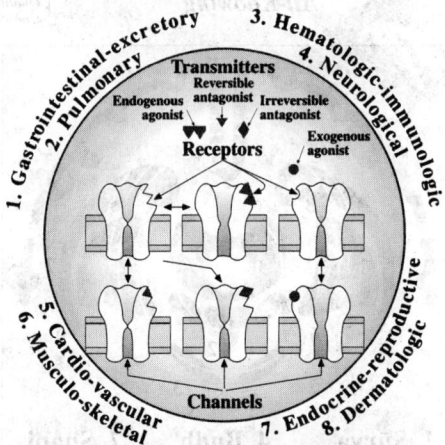

This figure shows how transmitters activate the receptors and lead to a transformation at the end-organ level. The transmitter operates like a key that fits in a specific lock and allows the opening of the door or channel. The receptors are located on the surface of the cells in the organ systems, summarized here in 8 categories corresponding to the 8 chapters of Chhand. The 24 most prominent transmitters, together with about 100 less prominent ones, relate to the 24 main metres and to approximately 100 secondary metres in the literature of Chhand.

144

JYOTISH — Vedic Term

**Basal Ganglia (9 components),
Cerebral Cortex (12 subdivisions),
Cranial Nerves (12 nerves),
and Brain Stem (27 groups of nuclei)** — Physiological Term

All-Knowing — Quality of Consciousness

1. Sūrya	4. Budh	7. Shani
2. Chandra	5. Guru	8. Rāhu
3. Mangal	6. Shukra	9. Ketu

This figure shows the 9 *Grahas* (planets) as they relate to the different parts of the basal ganglia, thalamus, and hypothalamus. [The 12 *Bhavas* (houses) correspond to 12 respective cortical areas; the 12 *Rashis* (signs) correspond to the 12 cranial nerves; and the 27 *Nakshatras* (asterisms) correspond to the 27 mono-aminergic groups of nuclei of the brain stem (these are not shown in this figure).]

Vedic Term — **NYĀYA** 145

Physiological Term — **Thalamus**
(5 sections, with 16 nuclei)

Quality of Consciousness — *Decisive and Distinguishing*

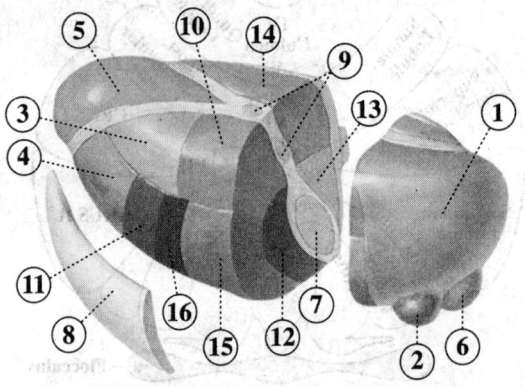

This figure shows the 16 nuclei of the thalamus corresponding to the 16 aspects of Nyāya. These are grouped in 5 sections corresponding to the 5 chapters of Nyāya.

VAISHESHIK

Cerebellum
(10 lobules of 2 divisions each and 370 gyri)
Specific

Vedic Term
Physiological Term
Quality of Consciousness

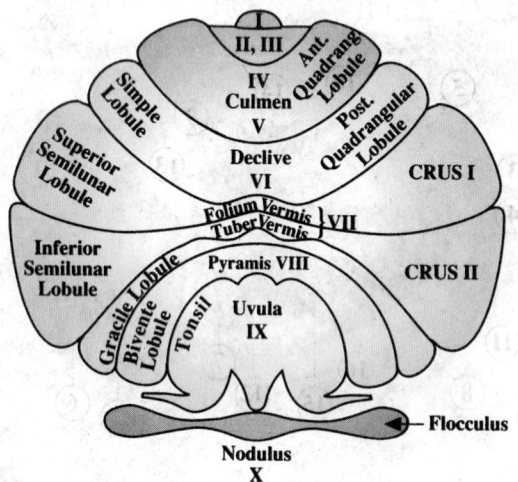

This figure shows the 10 lobules of the cerebellum divided into 2 sections (right and left) corresponding to the 10 chapters of Vaisheshik, which have 2 divisions each and comprise a total of 370 *Sūtra*. These are related to the (about) 370 small gyri of the cerebellum.

Vedic Term — **SĀMKHYA**

Physiological Term — **Types of Neuronal Activity**
(within the 6 layers of the cortex; 25 different types)

Quality of Consciousness — *Enumerating*

147

6 layers of the Cerebral Cortex

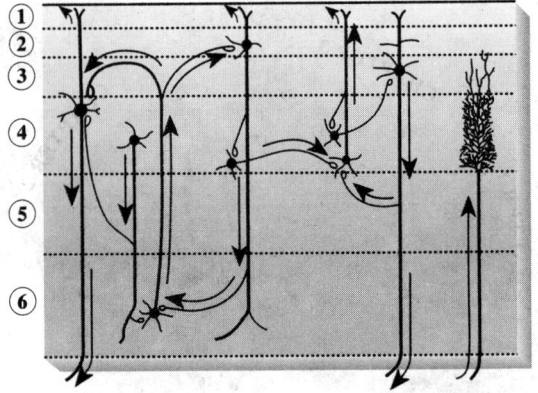

① ② ③ ④ ⑤ ⑥

This figure shows the 6 layers of the cerebral cortex corresponding to the 6 chapters of Sāmkhya. The various types of neuronal activity are illustrated in the figure by various incoming, integrating, and outgoing fibres with arrows showing the direction of flow of information. These can be classified into 25 categories corresponding to the 25 values of Sāmkhya.

148

YOGA — *Vedic Term*

Association Fibres of the Cerebral Cortex
(4 lobes with 51, 55, 55, and 34 long and short fasciculi, divided on the basis of the overlying gyri) — *Physiological Term*

Unifying — *Quality of Consciousness*

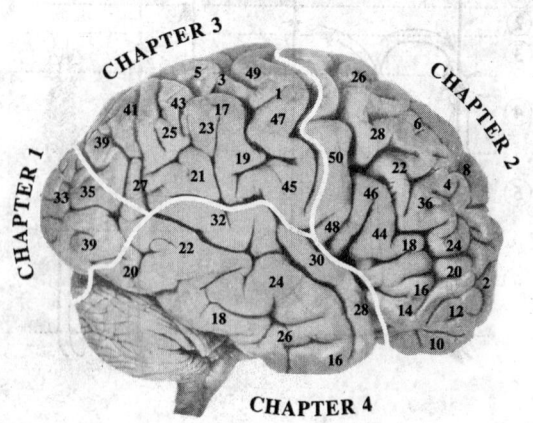

This figure shows a right lateral view of the brain with its 4 lobes and the locations of the 4 chapters of Yoga and the *Sūtra* in each chapter corresponding to each of the cortical gyri (folds) within these lobes.

Vedic Term: **KARMA MĪMĀMSĀ** 149

Physiological Term: **Central Nervous System**
(12 divisions with 60 subdivisions)

Quality of Consciousness: *Analysing*

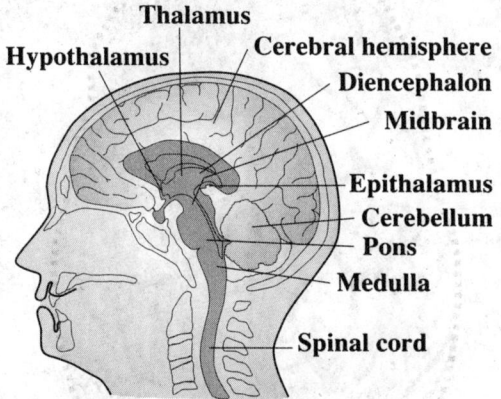

This figure shows some of the 12 divisions and 60 subdivisions of the central nervous system corresponding to the 12 chapters and 60 *Pāda* of Karma Mīmāmsā.

150

VEDĀNT] *Vedic Term*
**Integrated Functioning of the Central Nervous System
(including the 4 lobes of the cortex
and the 16 nuclei of the thalamus)**] *Physiological Term*
I-ness or Being] *Quality of Consciousness*

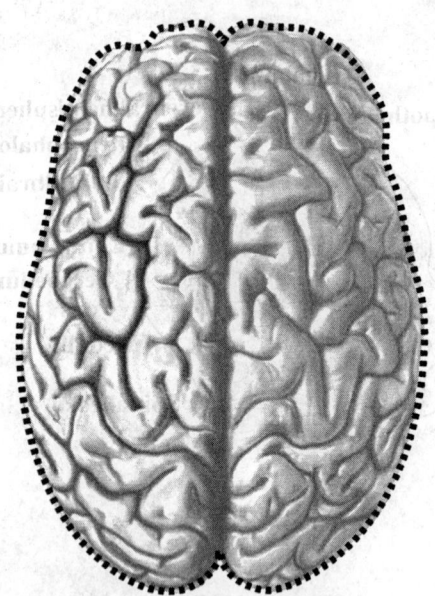

This figure shows a top view of the brain. Layer 1 of the cerebral cortex covers the surface of the brain. This layer corresponds to the holistic quality of Vedānt.

Vedic Term — # CHARAK SAṀHITĀ 151
Physiological Term — **Mesodermal Tissues and Organs**
Quality of Consciousness — *Holding Together, Nourishing and Supporting*

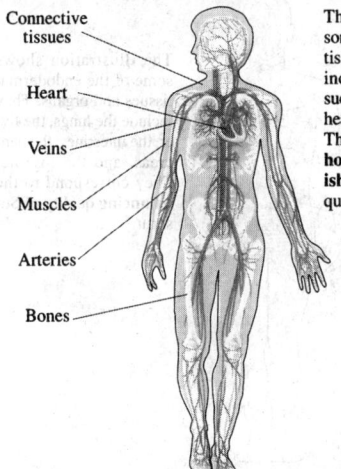

- Connective tissues
- Heart
- Veins
- Muscles
- Arteries
- Bones

The illustration shows some of the mesodermal tissues and organs. They include connective tissues, muscles, bones, the heart, arteries, and veins. They correspond to the **holding together**, **nourishing**, and **supporting** qualities of Charak.

Charak Saṁhitā represents the **holding together** of dynamism and silence. Its quality is **nourishing** and **supporting**. In the physiology it corresponds with all the tissues and organs formed by the embryologic mesoderm. From the mesoderm are formed the skeleton, muscles, and connective tissues, which hold the different parts of the body together and give support to the whole physiology. The heart and blood vessels are also formed by the mesoderm. They act as the basic **holding together**, **nourishing**, and **supporting** values, which are also qualities of Charak. The divisions and subdivisions of Charak Saṁhitā correspond to the basic organization and structure of the mesodermal tissues and organs.

152

SUSHRUT SAṀHITĀ
Endodermal Tissues and Organs
Balancing

] Vedic Term
] Physiological Term
] Quality of Consciousness

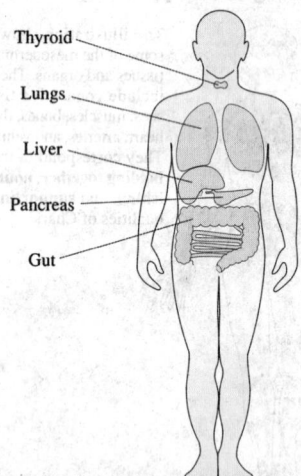

- Thyroid
- Lungs
- Liver
- Pancreas
- Gut

The illustration shows some of the endodermal tissues and organs. They include the lungs, the liver, the intestines, the pancreas, and the thyroid. They correspond to the **balancing** quality of Sushrut.

Sushrut Saṁhitā represents the quality of **balancing**. In the physiology it corresponds to the tissues and organs formed by the endoderm. They include the lungs, the liver, the intestines, the pancreas, the thyroid, and the thymus. These organs maintain different aspects of the physiology in **balance**. For example: through the lungs oxygen/carbon dioxide **balance** is maintained in the tissues; the gut glands and the liver **balance** the amount of nutrients that are needed in the blood and tissues; the pancreas **balances** the amount of sugar, and the thyroid keeps metabolism in proper **balance**. The divisions and subdivisions of Sushrut Saṁhitā correspond to the basic organization and structure of the endodermal tissues and organs.

Vedic Term	# VĀGBHATT SAMHITĀ	153
Physiological Term	**Ectodermal Tissues and Organs**	
Quality of Consciousness	*Communicating and Eloquent*	

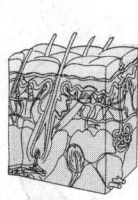

Skin

The illustration shows some of the ectodermal tissues and organs. The nervous system and skin fulfil the role of **communication** and **eloquence**.

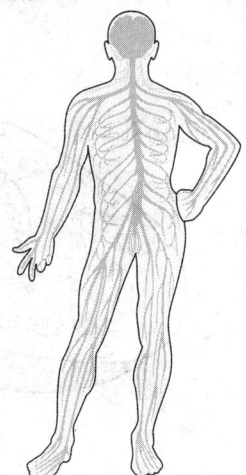

Nervous System

Vāgbhatt Samhitā represents the quality of **communication** and **eloquence**. In the physiology it corresponds to the tissues and organs of ectodermal origin. They include the entire nervous system, the skin, and the lens of the eye. The nervous system is the seat of all **communication** and **eloquence**. The skin is the interface with the outside world; it receives through its receptors information about the environment and therefore also plays an important role in **communication**. The divisions and subdivisions of Vāgbhatt Samhitā correspond to the basic organization and structure of the ectodermal tissues and organs.

BHĀVA-PRAKĀSH SAMHITĀ
Cell Nucleus
Enlightening

Vedic Term
Physiological Term
Quality of Consciousness

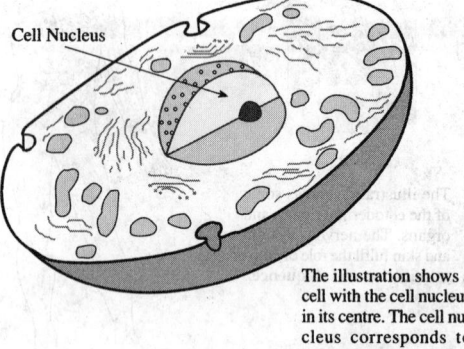

The illustration shows a cell with the cell nucleus in its centre. The cell nucleus corresponds to Bhāva-Prakāsh Samhitā.

Bhāva-Prakāsh Samhitā represents the **enlightening** quality of consciousness. It is represented in the physiology by the cell nucleus. The cell nucleus contains the genetic material which guides all cellular activity and growth. The DNA in the cell nucleus contains all the knowledge about all cycles, cell shape, specification, and response to various conditions. It maintains the activity of the cell in harmony with all other cells. It ensures orderliness and balance. This is the '**enlightening**' quality of the cell nucleus for all cells and tissues of the body.

Vedic Term: # SHĀRNGADHAR SAMHITĀ

155

Physiological Term: **Cytoplasm and Cytoskeleton**

Quality of Consciousness: *Synthesizing*

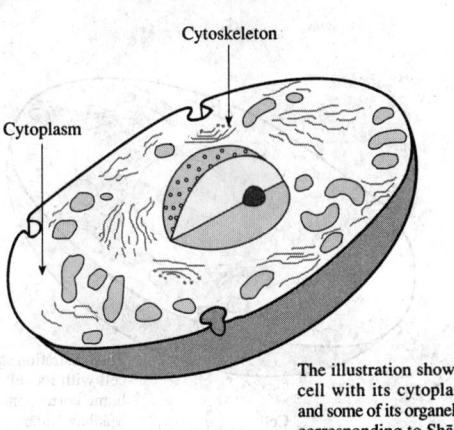

The illustration shows a cell with its cytoplasm and some of its organelles corresponding to Shārngadhar Samhitā.

Shārngadhar Samhitā represents the **synthesizing** value of consciousness. In the physiology, it is represented by the cell cytoplasm and cytoskeleton. The subcellular organelles include the endoplasmic reticulum, which is responsible for membrane **synthesis**, the **synthesis** of proteins and lipids for cell organelles, and for export and detoxication reactions. Other organelles are also involved in various aspects of cell metabolism, energy conservation, and modification and sorting of protein.

MĀDHAV NIDĀN SAMHITĀ
Cell Membrane
Detecting and Recognizing

Vedic Term
Physiological Term
Quality of Consciousness

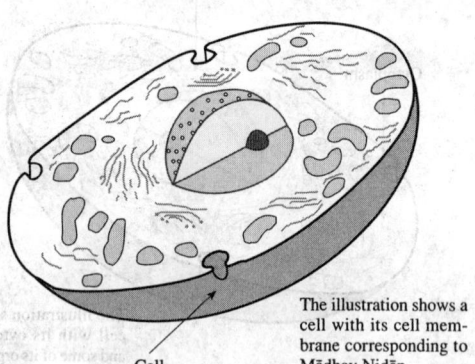

The illustration shows a cell with its cell membrane corresponding to Mādhav Nidān.

Cell Membrane

Mādhav Nidān Saṁhitā represents the **detecting** and **recognizing** values of consciousness. It is represented in the physiology by the cell membrane. The cell membrane contains the receptors of the cell, which detect and recognize molecules coming into contact with the cell. The cell evaluates the significance of these molecules for its activity via the response generated by the cell membrane receptors. This **detecting** and **recognizing** specialty of the cell membrane makes it equivalent to the **detecting** and **recognizing** qualities of Mādhav Nidān.

	SMRITI	157
Vedic Term		
Physiological Term	**Memory Systems and Reflexes** (36 cranial nerve nuclei)	
Quality of Consciousness	*Memory*	

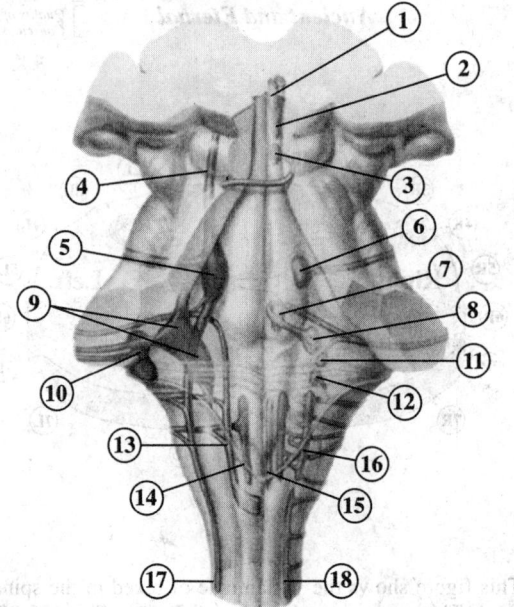

This figure shows the 18 nuclei of the cranial nerves. They correspond to the 18 Smriti.

Note: All the nuclei are bilateral but they are shown here only on one side. The 18 nuclei on the opposite side correspond to the 18 Upa-Smriti.

158   PURĀṆ

Great Intermediate Net
(about 400,000 neurons to each motor neuron; 18 laminae of rexed; 36 cranial nerve nuclei; 36 autonomic ganglia)

Ancient and Eternal

| *Vedic Term* |
| *Physiological Term* |
| *Quality of Consciousness* |

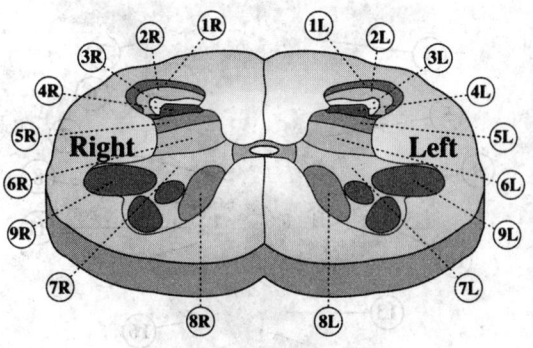

This figure shows the 18 laminae of rexed in the spinal cord. They correspond to the 18 Purāṇ. The 400,000 neurons in the 'great intermediate net' for each motor neuron relate to the 400,000 verses of Purāṇ. The 18 Purāṇ and the 18 Upa-Purāṇ also correspond to the 36 nuclei (18 right and 18 left) of the cranial nerves, as well as to the 36 autonomic ganglia on each side of the spinal cord.

Vedic Term — **ITIHĀS**

159

Physiological Term — **Voluntary Motor and Sensory Projections**

Quality of Consciousness — *Blossoming of Totality*

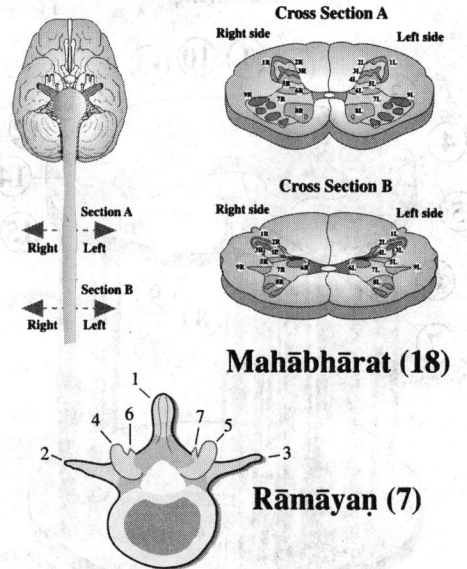

Mahābhārat (18)

Rāmāyaṇ (7)

This figure shows two cross sections of the spinal cord at two different levels. For illustration, the laminae of Rexed are shaded and numbered within the grey matter. Each lamina of Rexed corresponds to a specific book of the Mahābhārat.

Rāmāyaṇ has 7 chapters. They correspond to the 7 spinal processes (two superior, two inferior, two lateral and one posterior). There are also 7 cervical vertebrae which hold and support the neck and the head. They could also be seen to correspond to the 7 chapters of Rāmāyaṇ.

160 BRĀHMAṆA
Descending Tracts of the Central Nervous System
(15-18 main tracts)
Structuring

Vedic Term

Physiological Term

Quality of Consciousness

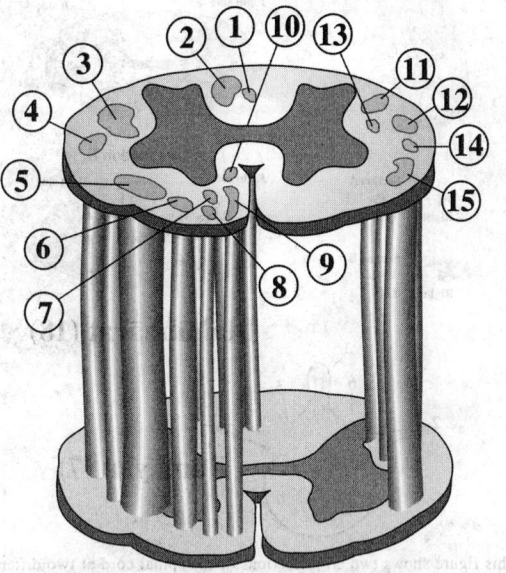

This figure shows the 15 main descending tracts. They correspond to the 15 main Brāhmaṇa. Other descending tracts corresponding to the three remaining Brāhmaṇa (not shown in this picture) are the corticotectal, corticopontine, and corticobulbar tracts.

Vedic Term	**ĀRAṆYAK**
Physiological Term	**Fasciculi Proprii** (6 divisions)
Quality of Consciousness	***Stirring***

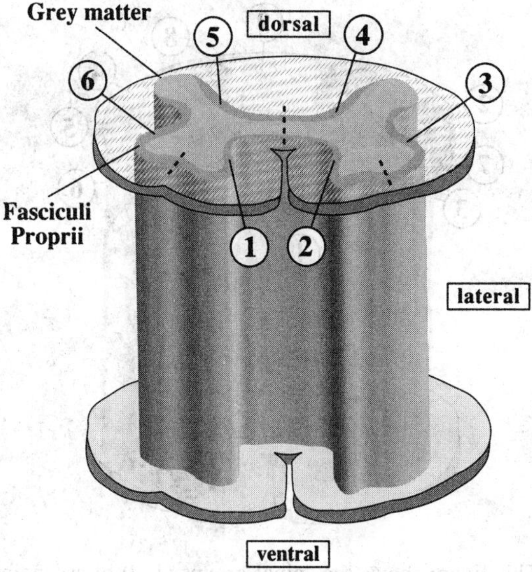

161

Grey matter

Fasciculi Proprii

dorsal

lateral

ventral

① ② ③ ④ ⑤ ⑥

This figure shows the 6 sets of fasciculi proprii around the grey matter of the spinal cord. They correspond to the 6 books of Āraṇyak.

162 UPANISHAD

**Ascending Tracts of the
Central Nervous System**
(10–15 main tracts with a large number of
possible combinations of ascending fibres)

Transcendental and Self-Referral

Vedic Term

Physiological Term

Quality of Consciousness

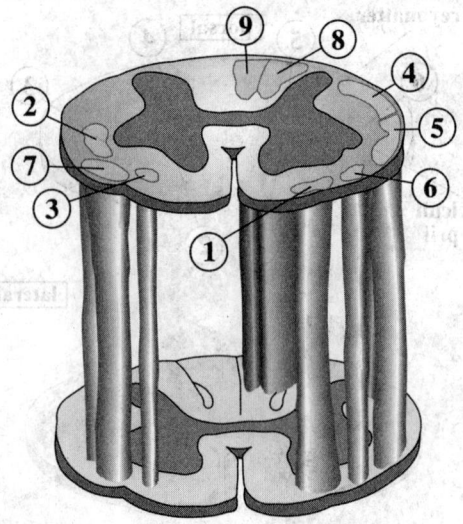

This figure shows the spinal groups (1–9) of ascending tracts carrying the inputs of sensory information from the periphery. Tracts carrying special sensory modalities such as hearing, sight, taste, and smell are not shown here. Together these tracts correspond to the main 10–15 Upanishad.

ṚK VEDA PRĀTISHĀKHYA

Vedic Term

A Granular Plexiform Layer—Horizontal Communication—Cerebral Cortex Layer 1

Physiological Term

All-Pervading

Quality of Consciousness

Cerebral cortex layer 1

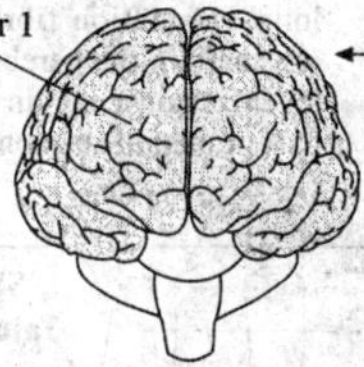

This illustration shows the cerebral cortex on the surface of which is layer 1. The lower part of this illustration highlights layer 1 among the 6 layers of the cortex.

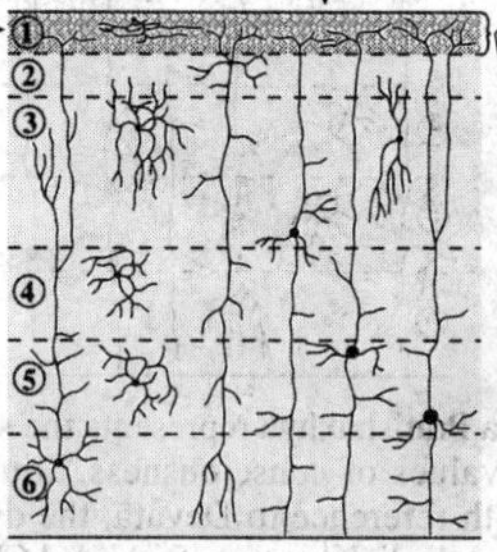

Layer 1
A granular plexiform layer—horizontal communication

Ṛk Veda Prātishākhya *Belongs to Ṛk Veda*

Ṛk Veda Prātishākhya is the holistic, transcendental aspect of WHOLENESS itself—totally integrated, point in infinity and infinity in every point—it represents Unity, the **all-pervading** field of consciousness. Layer 1 of the cerebral cortex does not send projections outside itself; it receives projections from all other layers. It is self-referral WHOLENESS corresponding to the Ṛk Veda Prātishākhya.

164 SHUKL-YAJUR-VEDA PRĀTISHĀKHYA

Vedic Term

Corticocortical Fibres, Cerebral Cortex Layer 2

Physiological Term

Silencing, Sharing, and Spreading

Quality of Consciousness

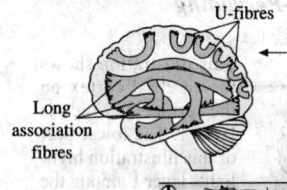

The illustration shows the corticocortical fibres (U-fibres and long association fibres). They originate in the cerebral cortex layer 2 highlighted in the lower part of this illustration.

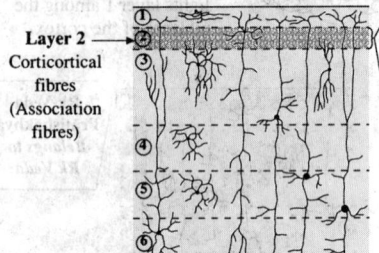

Shukl-Yajur-Veda Prātishākhya *Belongs to Yajur-Veda*

Shukl-Yajur-Veda Prātishākhya represents the **silencing**, **sharing**, and **spreading** values of consciousness. Yajur-Veda represents WHOLENESS with reference to Devatā, the dynamic quality of observing, which is the link between Ṛishi and Chhandas—between the knower and the known. It corresponds in the physiology to the processing systems. The higher order cognitive level of this interconnecting and processing aspect of physiological activity resides in the cerebral cortex in layers 2 and 3. Neurons in layer 2 of the cerebral cortex send their axons to other cortical layers interconnecting them. They have the ability to **silence**, **share**, and **spread** noise and unwanted information. Layer 2 corresponds to the Shukl-Yajur-Veda Prātishākhya.

Vedic Term — # KRISHN-YAJUR-VEDA 165
PRĀTISHĀKHYA (*Taittirīya*)
Physiological Term — ## Commisural and Corticocortical Fibres, Cerebral Cortex Layer 3
Quality of Consciousness — ### *Omnipresent*

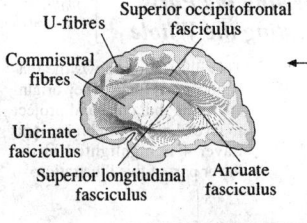

Labels (upper brain): U-fibres, Superior occipitofrontal fasciculus, Commisural fibres, Uncinate fasciculus, Superior longitudinal fasciculus, Arcuate fasciculus

The illustration shows the commisural fibres of the corpus callosum and various corticocortical fibres. They originate in the cerebral cortex layer 3 highlighted in the lower part of this illustration.

Layer 3 — Commisural and corticocortical fibres (Association fibres)

Krishn-Yajur-Veda Prātishākhya (*Taittirīya*) *Belongs to Yajur-Veda*

Krishn-Yajur-Veda Prātishākhya represents the **omnipresent** value of consciousness. Layer 3 of the cerebral cortex contains cells whose projections are spread via the commisural and corticocortical fibres to all areas of the cortex. The commisural fibres cross from one side of the brain to the other connecting distant cortical layers. They therefore are a wide-range integrating and processing set of fibres within the self-referral nature of the activity of the nervous system. They have a quality of **omnipresence**. Layer 3 therefore corresponds to the Krishn-Yajur-Veda Prātishākhya.

SĀMA VEDA PRĀTISHĀKHYA
(*Pushpa Sūtram*)
Thalamocortical Fibres, Cerebral Cortex Layer 4
Unmanifesting the Parts but Manifesting the Whole

Vedic Term

Physiological Term

Quality of Consciousness

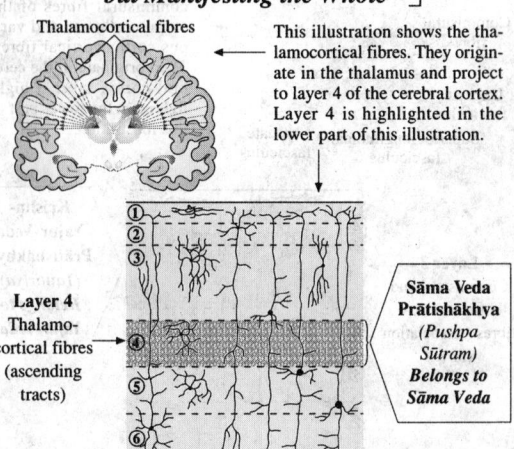

This illustration shows the thalamocortical fibres. They originate in the thalamus and project to layer 4 of the cerebral cortex. Layer 4 is highlighted in the lower part of this illustration.

Layer 4 Thalamocortical fibres (ascending tracts)

Sāma Veda Prātishākhya (*Pushpa Sūtram*) Belongs to Sāma Veda

Sāma Veda Prātishākhya corresponds to the **unmanifesting** and **manifesting** values of consciousness. Sāma Veda represents WHOLENESS with reference to Ṛishi, the observer value. It corresponds in the physiology to the sensory systems. The integration of sensory input into higher order perception in the cerebral cortex, **manifesting** WHOLENESS, allows WHOLENESS to emerge while **unmanifesting** the specific aspects of sensory experience. The layer of the cerebral cortex which receives specific afferent (incoming) sensory inputs is layer 4. This layer corresponds to the Sāma Veda Prātishākya.

Vedic Term	# ATHARVA VEDA PRĀTISHĀKHYA
Physiological Term	**Cortico-striate, -tectal, -spinal Fibres** **Cerebral Cortex Layer 5**
Quality of Consciousness	*Unfolding*

167

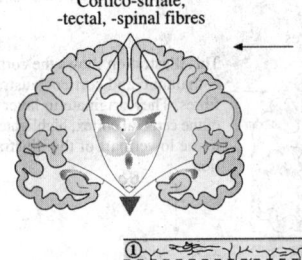

Cortico-striate, -tectal, -spinal fibres

This illustration shows the corticostriate, corticotectal, and corticospinal fibres. They originate in layer 5 of the cerebral cortex, highlighted in the lower part of the illustration.

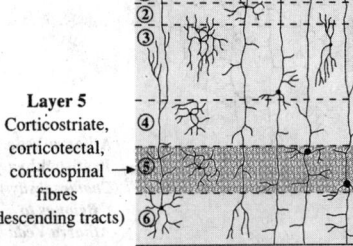

Layer 5 Corticostriate, corticotectal, corticospinal fibres (descending tracts)

Atharva Veda Prātishākhya *Belongs to Atharva Veda*

Atharva Veda Prātishākya represents the **unfolding** quality of consciousness. Atharva Veda represents WHOLENESS with reference to Chhandas, the observed value. It corresponds in the physiology to the motor systems. The highest order planning and initiation of motor activity reside in the cerebral cortex. Layer 5 of the cerebral cortex contains the neuronal cells called pyramidal cells which send their axons outside the cortex and brain to **unfold** motor activity. Layer 5 corresponds to the Atharva Veda Prātishākhya.

168 ATHARVA VEDA PRĀTISHĀKHYA
(*Chaturadhyāyi*)
Corticothalamic and Corticoclaustral Fibres, Cerebral Cortex Layer 6
Dissolving

Vedic Term

Physiological Term

Quality of Consciousness

Corticothalamic, Corticoclaustral fibres

This illustration shows the corticothalamic and corticoclaustral fibres. They originate in layer 6 of the cerebral cortex, highlighted in the lower part of the illustration.

Layer 6
Corticothalamic and corticoclaustral fibres (descending tracts)

Atharva Veda Prātishākhya (*Chaturadhyāyi*) **Belongs to Atharva Veda**

Atharva Veda Prātishākhya (*Chaturadhyāyi*) represents the **dissolving** value of consciousness. Atharva Veda represents WHOLENESS with reference to Chhandas, the observed value. It corresponds in the physiology to the motor systems. Layer 6 of the cerebral cortex also contains pyramidal cells. They send axons to the thalamus and keep its input in balance by **dissolving** unwanted inputs. Layer 6 of the cerebral cortex corresponds to the Atharva Veda Prātishākhya (*Chaturadhyāyi*).

ern science and ancient Vedic Science, and has also substantiated that part of every religion which says that man is created in the image of God, creation is created by the Will of God—Natural Law; everything everywhere is the expression of the Will of God—Natural Law:

ईशा वास्यमिदं सर्वं यत्किञ्च जगत्यां जगत्
तेन त्यक्तेन भुञ्जीथा मा गृधः कस्य स्विद्धनम्

Īshā vāsyam idam sarvam
yat kim-cha jagatyām jagat
ten tyakten bhunjīthā
mā gṛidhaḥ kasya swid dhanam
(Īshāvāsyā Upanishad, 1)

All this (creation) is the dwelling of the Administrator, the Creator.

This discovery of the physiology in terms of the structure of consciousness, as available in the Vedic Literature, has bridged the four-hundred-year-old gap between religion[*] and science.

---

[*] The purpose of mentioning the implications of science and religion to the field of management satisfies the faith of every individual, whether he has faith in science or in any religion, and gives him the experience and intellectual understanding of the holistic and specific values of Natural Law.

Supreme Quality of Management
Action from the Settled State of Mind

It is interesting to analyse self-referral performance—action from the settled state of mind—action from Transcendental Consciousness—action in silence.

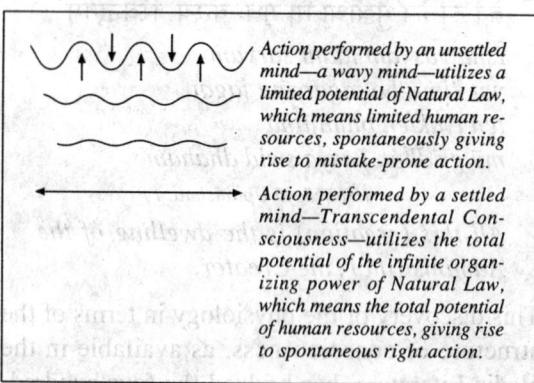

Action performed by an unsettled mind—a wavy mind—utilizes a limited potential of Natural Law, which means limited human resources, spontaneously giving rise to mistake-prone action.

Action performed by a settled mind—Transcendental Consciousness—utilizes the total potential of the infinite organizing power of Natural Law, which means the total potential of human resources, giving rise to spontaneous right action.

The figure shows that when motion is in waves its speed is less because the direction is up, down, and sideways. In a straight line the motion is direct and therefore faster.

A straight line represents infinite frequency, the field of silence, where energy is not dissipated in up and down directions—it directly hits the target.

The Principle of Least Action (Physics) is only realized on this level of action in SILENCE, where action yields maximum results with minimum effort. Minimum effort is available in silent wakefulness where consciousness is self-referral—where consciousness is the fully awake, fully alert field of the infinite organizing power of Natural Law. The full potential of intelligence is available in this quality of action in silence.

The silent level of consciousness is a field of all possibilities where the total potential of the organizing power of Natural Law is always fully awake, fully alert. It is this silent, omnipresent level of Natural Law that spontaneously governs the universe. This is the quality*of action that should be developed in everyone. Education should train the mind and body of everyone so that no one encounters stress, strain, and problems in life.

---

* The development of higher states of consciousness gives a vision of greater creativity. Greater creativity
Continued on page 313 ...

Action in silence ('Field Effect', Physics) is action from the level of infinite correlation—from the level of the 'field', where the total energy of Natural Law is utilized to fulfil the intention.

Action propelled from this level of silence consumes least energy and utilizes the total organizing power of Natural Law (Principle of Least Action) to hit the target with maximum speed and least resistance.

This is skill in action—this action in silence that provides automation to administration is not only upheld by the objective approach of modern science (Physics, Chemistry, Mathematics, Biology, Physiology, Quantum Cosmology, etc.) but is also upheld by ancient Vedic Science—Ṛk Veda:

यतीनां ब्रह्मा भवति सारथिः

Yatīnāṁ Brahmā bhavati sārathiḥ (Ṛk Veda, 1.158.6)
Those established in the silent singularity of self-referral consciousness motivate the infinite organizing power of the total potential of Natural Law to be their charioteer—
the infinite organizing power of Natural Law upholds their thought and action—the evolutionary power of Natural Law works for them, rendering automation in administration.

योगस्थः कुरु कर्माणि
Yogasthaḥ kuru karmāṇi (Bhagavad-Gītā, 2.48)
Established in Yoga (Unity), perform action.

योगः कर्मसु कौशलम्
Yogaḥ karmasu kaushalam (Bhagavad-Gītā, 2.50)
Yoga is skill in action.

क्रियासिद्धिः सत्त्वे भवति महतां नोपकरणे
Kriyā siddhiḥ sattwe bhavati mahatām nopakaraṇe
Success comes through Sattwa (purity)—pure, self-referral consciousness—which being the source of everything, contains within itself all that is needed for the fulfilment of any desire.

Transcendental Meditation

My Transcendental Meditation is a simple, natural, effortless procedure whereby the mind easily and naturally arrives at the source of thought, the settled state of mind—Transcendental Consciousness—pure consciousness, self-referral consciousness, which is the source of all creative processes.

This process can be likened to a river which naturally and effortlessly flows onto the ocean and gains the status of the ocean.

Transcendental Meditation is practised for 15 to 20 minutes in the morning and evening, while sitting comfortably with the eyes closed. During this technique the individual's awareness settles down and experiences a unique state of restful alertness; as the body becomes deeply relaxed, the mind transcends all mental activity to experience the simplest form of awareness—Transcendental Consciousness—where consciousness is open to itself. This is the self-referral state of consciousness.

The experience of Transcendental Consciousness develops the individual's latent creative potential, while dissolving accumulated stress and fatigue through the deep rest gained during the practice. This experience enlivens within one's awareness creativity, dynamism, orderliness, and organizing power, which results in increasing effectiveness and success in daily life.

Transcendental Meditation can be easily learnt by anyone. People of all levels of intelligence,[*] belonging to all ages, belonging to all cultures, religions, and educational backgrounds in countries throughout the world practise the technique.

The Transcendental Meditation Programme is the most direct way for the fulfilment of the supreme philosophy of life, where the individual lives life in full enlightenment, and where the individual breathes life in Cosmic Reality.

As the practical aspect of the supreme philosophy of life, my Transcendental Meditation is most natural, and as such it is universally applicable for the well-being of the individual and society as a whole.

---

[*] Since the beginning of the Transcendental Meditation Movement in 1959, 40,000 teachers of Transcendental Meditation have been trained throughout the world.

Transcendental Meditation renders all aspects of life according to Natural Law. Its application in the fields of politics, economy, religion, and culture of every country is so rewarding that it has started to bring a new wave of excellence to lead the present civilization to the height of perfection.

The benefits of Transcendental Meditation are so many and so great that it has been our delight to launch a programme for the complete transformation of life on earth — Heaven on Earth. How is Transcendental Meditation able to accomplish this overall enrichment of life?

Firstly, Transcendental Meditation is the Technology of Consciousness, which is the most basic element of life—the home of all the Laws of Nature. Refer to the *Ṛicho Akshare* verse of Ṛk Veda *(Ṛk Veda, 1.164.39)*, which explains how Transcendental Meditation (*Parame vyoman*) unfolds the creative genius (*Yasmin Devā*) of the self-referral state of intelligence—the home of all the Laws of Nature (*Ṛicho Ak-kshare*)—and inspires the Laws of Nature to uphold all thought, speech, and action: support of Natural Law increases in daily life with regular practice.

Secondly, it eliminates the most basic cause of all stress and strain. Everyone lives his life through the cycles of routine work, whether he is a student, a working adult, or retired—the whole population is living life through routine work, and routine work in daily life does not provide an opportunity for the full expression of Creative Intelligence.

This lack of opportunity to display creativity causes frustration and becomes the basis of all anti-social behaviour.

Transcendental Meditation helps the awareness to transcend boundaries and go beyond the field of limitations; this is how Transcendental Meditation, providing the opportunity to create unboundedness, infinity, eternity, satisfies the inner creativity and inner genius of life by providing an opportunity for the full expression of Creative Intelligence.

The daily opportunity for the individual's awareness to go beyond boundaries (through Transcendental Meditation) neutralizes the rigidity caused by the boundaries of the daily routine.

Thirdly, the marvel of Transcendental Meditation is that both of these above-mentioned values—the blossoming of creativity, and dissolution of stress and strain—are achieved in one stroke.

Transcendental Meditation
The Promoter of Evolution

This means that Transcendental Meditation is capable of promoting the process of evolution of life. Evolution or growth is brought about by two processes simultaneously—the present state must be destroyed and during the process of destruction, creation of a new state must be brought about; creation and destruction—two opposite processes are held in balance in order

---

* परित्राणाय साधूनां विनाशाय च दुष्कृताम्
  धर्मसंस्थापनार्थाय संभवामि युगे युगे
  Paritrāṇāya sādhūnāṁ vināshāya cha dushkṛitām
  Continued on page 313 ...

* विषया विनिवर्त्तन्ते निराहारस्य देहिनः
  रसवर्जं रसोऽप्यस्य परं दृष्ट्वा निवर्तते
  Vishayā vinivartante nirāhārasya dehinaḥ
  Continued on page 315 ...

* Transcendental Meditation is a must for everyone in the world because the benefits that it produces in
  Continued on page 316 ...

that evolution is perpetually maintained.

Transcendental Meditation is the promoter of evolution through which life is ever sustained in progress. Transcendental Meditation produces Transcendental Consciousness—self-referral consciousness—in which all transformations take place.

We have seen in Physics that the Unified Field of all the Laws of Nature is a state of self-referral consciousness; and we have seen in Chemistry that the transition state is the state of self-referral consciousness. We have seen in Mathematics that the consciousness of the mathematician is the source of all order, and that the Null Set is the self-perpetuating source (self-referral consciousness) of all sets. We have also clearly seen that in Regulatory Physiology the self-referral activity of the homoeostatic feedback system constantly maintains balance in the physiology.

Transcendental Meditation, the Technology of Consciousness, the technology of self-referral consciousness, is therefore the technology of the Unified Field in Physics, the technology of the

Transition State in Chemistry, the technology of the Integrating Centre in Regulatory Physiology, and the technology of the Null Set, the source of all sets, in Mathematics; it is Vedic Mathematics, the technology of Natural Law, the structuring dynamics of creation; it is the technology for enlivening the structure of the Veda—it is the mathematics of consciousness that enlivens the structuring dynamics of creation and evolution.

Transcendental Meditation Enjoyable Exercise of Vedic Mathematics

Transcendental Meditation is the programme of Vedic Mathematics because it enlivens and utilizes the holistic value of Natural Law to materialize an all-directional effect in all fields of space and time. It is this theme of Vedic Mathematics available through Transcendental Meditation that promotes absolute order from the common basis of all activity in the universe—the self-referral, unified field of consciousness.

Transcendental Meditation, the Technology of Consciousness, the technology of self-referral consciousness, enlivens in the field of consciousness the total Constitution of the Universe—the total potential of Natural Law—the structuring dynamics of creation available as the intelligence and organizing power in every cell of the human physiology.

To develop expertise in the field of Vedic Mathematics the guideline is:

निस्त्रैगुण्यो भवार्जुन
Nistrai-guṇyo bhav-Arjuna
(Bhagavad-Gītā, 2.45)
Be without the three Guṇas, O Arjuna!

योगस्थः कुरु कर्माणि
Yogasthaḥ kuru karmāṇi
(Bhagavad-Gītā, 2.48)
Established in the Self, perform action.

सहजं कर्म कौन्तेय
Sahajaṁ karma Kaunteya
(Bhagavad-Gītā, 18.48)
Perform natural duty because unfathomable is the course of action.

---

* ... so that you do not end up with a lotus when you desire a rose.

These are the three requirements to gain expertise in Vedic Mathematics, which means gaining mastery over Natural Law.

That means:

1. Gain Transcendental Consciousness—self-referral consciousness. For this, practise Transcendental Meditation twice daily.

2. Act from the most settled, silent, coherent state of mind—act from the peaceful state of the mind, the level of Transcendental Consciousness.

   For this, optimize brain functioning through the daily practice of the TM-Sidhi Programme. This will bring the support of Natural Law for all thought, speech, and action.

3. Support of Natural Law will render all thought, speech, and action free from stress and strain—life will naturally progress to greater levels of achievement and fulfilment; life will naturally be easy, without problems or failures.

Any action performed from self-referral consciousness is supported by the invincible power of Natural Law. Gaining the ability to spontaneously enjoy the support of Natural Law is gaining expertise in Vedic Mathematics, which opens the door of all possibilities in daily life.

In conclusion, skill in Vedic Mathematics requires broadening the mind by simply expanding the awareness and developing infinite creativity through regular practice of Transcendental Meditation.

Through Transcendental Meditation the awareness of the individual gains self-referral consciousness; it identifies with the self-referral state of consciousness, Saṁhitā level of consciousness, the field of pure intelligence—infinite Creative Intelligence—and through the self-referral dynamics of self-referral consciousness, the diversified state of the awareness of the individual realizes the concentrated power of Natural Law in its unified state, and through practice lives Natural Law in daily life. That is why it is a proven panacea for all good to everyone.

This is the reason why my Transcendental Meditation forms the central core of my Absolute Theory of Management, my Absolute Theory of

Government, my Absolute Theory of Education, my Absolute Theory of Health, my Absolute Theory of Defence, my Absolute Theory of Law and Order, my Absolute Theory of Rehabilitation, my Absolute Theory of Economics, and forms my central programme to transform our present civilization from an age of suffering and ignorance to an age of happiness and enlightenment—the Age of Enlightenment—Heaven on Earth.

This is the glorious vision of my Transcendental Meditation; this is the beautiful definition and all-encompassing scope of my Transcendental Meditation; this is the glimpse of the infinite potential of the infinite organizing power of pure knowledge available to everyone within himself through my Transcendental Meditation; this is the authentic achievement of Transcendental Meditation.

Transcendental Meditation is my one gift to the world for all good for everyone for millenniums to come.

This explains why Maharishi University of Management uses Transcendental Meditation (TM) as a means to develop perfect management, mastery of management, TIMELY MANAGEMENT (TM). Refer to page 79.

TM-Sidhi Programme

The TM-Sidhi Programme is an advanced aspect of Transcendental Meditation. It trains the individual to think and act from the level of Transcendental Consciousness, greatly enhancing the co-ordination between mind and body, and developing the ability to enliven Natural Law to support all avenues of life to fulfil one's desires.

Yogic Flying

Yogic Flying is a phenomenon created by a specific thought projected from Transcendental Consciousness, the Unified Field of Natural Law, the field of all possibilities. This is the simplest state of human consciousness, self-referral consciousness, which is easily accessible to anyone through Transcendental Meditation, and is enlivened through the TM-Sidhi Programme, which leads to Yogic Flying.

Yogic Flying demonstrates perfect mind-body co-ordination and is correlated with maximum

Continued on page 188 ...

EEG RESEARCH LOCATES THE SEAT O
BRAIN THROUGH THE TM-SIDI

Creating Coherence in World Consciou
in the Coherently Functioning

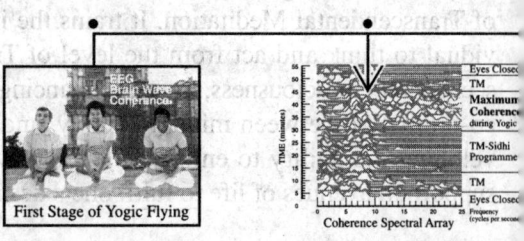

First Stage of Yogic Flying

Coherence Spectral Array

Optimum brain functioning, as indicated by maximum coherence (orderliness) in brainwave activity during the TM-Sidhi Programme of Yogic Flying, creates the perfect condition for the frictionless flow of awareness towards the fulfilment of its desire.

The Principle of Least Action, which governs all activity in Nature with mathematical precision and order and uses the skill of Natural Law to quietly accomplish everything, is available in its optimum value when brainwave coherence is maximum and awareness is in its simplest state—Transcendental Consciousness.

During the Yogic Flying technique, at the moment of maximum coherence in brainwave activity, the

ERFECT MANAGEMENT IN THE HUMAN
ROGRAMME OF YOGIC FLYING

s and Locating the Seat of World Peace
n Physiology of the Individual

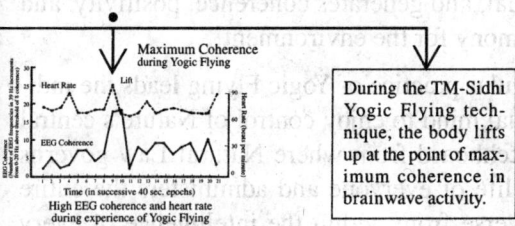

High EEG coherence and heart rate during experience of Yogic Flying

During the TM-Sidhi Yogic Flying technique, the body lifts up at the point of maximum coherence in brainwave activity.

body lifts up and begins to hop (the first stage of 'flying'). Simultaneously, the individual experiences waves of exhilaration and profound stabilization of the silent level of awareness. This enlivens the creative intelligence of Natural Law in the individual brain physiology.

As the practice advances, the increasing purity of body and mind results in thought and action more and more in accord with Natural Law—more and more in the evolutionary direction of Natural Law—all thought, speech, action, and behaviour naturally progressing in the evolutionary direction of Natural Law.

Continued on page 316 ...

coherence*, indicating maximum orderliness and integration of brain functioning. Even in the first stage of Yogic Flying, where the body lifts up in a series of short hops, this practice gives the experience of bubbling bliss for the individual, and generates coherence, positivity, and harmony for the environment.

Regular practice of Yogic Flying leads the individual mind to enjoy control of Nature's central switchboard from where Natural Law governs the life of everyone and administers the entire universe from within the intelligence of every grain of creation.

From this level of the total potential of Natural Law the individual can command all channels of Nature's infinite creativity and the invincible organizing power of Natural Law. Just as an order from the Prime Minister commands the total authority and resources of the nation for its implementation, similarly, any intention projected from the Unified Field of Natural Law commands the infinite organizing power of Natural Law for its immediate fulfilment.

---

*As measured by electroencephalograph (EEG).

The practice of Yogic Flying provides a practical demonstration of the ability to project thought from the Unified Field of Natural Law, and develops the ability to act spontaneously in accord with Natural Law for the fulfilment of any desire. The phenomenon of Yogic Flying proves that through my Transcendental Meditation and TM-Sidhi Programme, anyone can gain the ability to function from the simplest form of their own awareness and can develop mastery over Natural Law.

My TM-Sidhi Programme provides a direct entry to the full blossoming of the creative genius of everyone; it is a master key to open the field of higher states of consciousness, where one naturally lives life supported by the evolutionary power of Natural Law.

All parents, all teachers, and all governments should make these programmes available to the growing youth in order to save them from problems and suffering in life through the support of Natural Law.

Maharishi Effect

The *Maharishi Effect* is the phenomenon of the rise of coherence in the collective consciousness of any community.

The *Maharishi Effect* was discovered by social scientists in the U.S.A. in 1974 in four towns, where the number of people participating in the Transcendental Meditation Programme had reached one per cent of the town's population.

They noted that when one per cent of the town's population practised Transcendental Meditation, the trend of rising crime rate was reversed, indicating increasing order and harmony.

Research scientists named this phenomenon of rising coherence in the collective consciousness of the whole society the *Maharishi Effect*, because this was the realization of my promise to society made in the very early days of the Movement (1957).

The phenomenon of the *Maharishi Effect* (like the phenomenon of the Meissner* Effect in Phys-

Continued on page 192 ...

---

* A universal principle in Nature is that internally
Continued on page 318 ...

Maharishi Effect
Creating an Invincible Armour for the Nation

NATIONAL ARMOUR
An invincible border that makes the nation impenetrable to any harmful influence from the outside.

The *Maharishi Effect* refers to the growth of harmony in society resulting from the practice of Maharishi's Vedic Technology—the technology of Natural Law—by a small fraction of the population. When the influence of coherence generated by this technology reaches sufficient intensity, an integrated national consciousness is created. This in turn strengthens the cultural integrity of the nation by promoting life in accord with Natural Law. The result is the development of self-sufficiency and an invincible armour for the nation, which automatically repels any negative influence coming from outside.

Thus, the integrated state of national consciousness created by the *Maharishi Effect* produces a 'Meissner Effect' for the nation, rendering it impenetrable to external disorder.

ics) discovered by scientists has repeatedly verified that coherence in collective consciousness and positivity and harmony in national consciousness is produced by the group practice of my Transcendental Meditation. This has proved to be a formula to create irreversible world peace and Heaven on Earth—all good to everyone and non-good to no one—the basis of a coherent, integrated society and a perfect government.

The Extended Maharishi Effect[*]

In 1976, with the introduction of the more advanced TM-Sidhi Programme, including Yogic Flying, a more powerful effect was expected. The first major test of this prediction took place in 1978 during my Global Ideal Society Campaign in 108 countries: crime rate was reduced everywhere.

This global research demonstrated a new for-

---

[*] Over 40 independent research studies on the city, provincial, national, and international levels confirm that the *Maharishi Effect,* the *Extended Maharishi Effect,* and the *Global Maharishi Effect* improve the quality of life in society and the trends of life in the entire world.

mula: the square root of one per cent of a population practising Transcendental Meditation and the TM-Sidhi Programme, morning and evening together in one place, is sufficient to neutralize negative tendencies and promote positive trends throughout the whole population.

This much-reduced requirement—in many cases just a few hundred individuals practising my Vedic Technology of Transcendental Meditation, the TM-Sidhi Programme, and Yogic Flying to bring life in accordance with Natural Law for a whole nation—enabled this discovery to be repeatedly verified on the city, provincial, and national levels.

Global Maharishi Effect

The *Global Maharishi Effect* was created by the group practice of 7,000 Yogic Flyers—7,000 being approximately the square root of one per cent of the world's population.

The *Global Maharishi Effect* was witnessed during three large 'World Peace Assemblies' which were held over a period of two to three weeks in the U.S.A., Holland, and India.

The secret of the *Global Maharishi Effect* is the phenomenon known to Physics as the 'Field Effect', the effect of coherence and positivity produced from the field of infinite correlation—the self-referral field of least excitation of consciousness—the field of Transcendental Consciousness, which is basic to creation and permeates all life everywhere.

The greatest[*] demonstration of the *Global Maharishi Effect* so far was evidenced when the enmity between the two superpowers (Soviet Union and U.S.A.) ended in a friendly handshake (1988).

With this, the two-thousand-year-old gospel of suffering is soon coming to an end, and a new civilization, Vedic Civilization of enlightenment and fulfilment, is dawning.[+]

Many carefully controlled experiments on the

---

[*] The supreme demonstration of the *Global Maharishi Effect* will be when every sovereign government rises to invincibility through the PREVENTION WING of its military.

[+] Maharishi inaugurated the Dawn of the Age of Enlightenment in 1975, after the *Maharishi Effect* was discovered (1974).

Maharishi Effect, the *Extended Maharishi Effect*, and the *Global Maharishi Effect* have appeared in leading scientific* journals.

These studies have utilized the most advanced and rigorous research designs and statistical methodologies to precisely evaluate the effect of large coherence-creating groups on standard sociological measures of the quality of life in cities, provinces, nations, and the world.

These studies have rigorously demonstrated the power of the *Maharishi Effect* to a degree of certainty that is unparalleled in the sociological sciences, and even in the physical sciences. Thus the *Maharishi Effect*, the *Extended Maharishi Effect*, and the *Global Maharishi Effect* have been more extensively documented and thoroughly established than any other phenomenon in the field of scientific research. ***The Maharishi Effect in itself proves the existence of the Unified Field of Natural Law and man's ability to oper-***

---

* Including *Journal of Conflict Resolution*, *Journal of Crime and Justice*, *Social Indicators Research*, and *Journal of Mind and Behavior*.

⁺ Time series impact assessment analysis, a special case of Box-Jenkins transfer function analysis.

ate from this level of the field producing the 'Field Effect'—Maharishi Effect.

The *Maharishi Effect* is rising in the world. World consciousness is constantly being purified. Already a new awakening of freedom is being witnessed in the world. The transformation of political, economic, and social values is taking place in the whole world with a fast pace.

As the *Maharishi Effect* is purifying world consciousness, old principles that were guiding life in the age of ignorance are being replaced by new principles that will guide life in the dawning Age of Enlightenment in today's world.

The *Maharishi Effect* is giving rise to new knowledge and more useful programmes for betterment in life. An example of this is the recent discovery of the Veda and Vedic Literature in human consciousness and physiology, and my programme to create Vedic Universities, Vedic Schools, Āyur-Veda Universities, and Universities of Management in different parts of the world, and my world-wide programme to create a disease-free society and problem-free governments—Heaven on Earth.

Scientific Research on Transcendental Meditation, the TM-Sidhi Programme, and Yogic Flying in the Field of Management

Over 500 scientific studies on the Transcendental Meditation Programme have been conducted during the past thirty-seven years by researchers at more than 214 independent research institutions in 27 countries. These include Harvard Medical School; Princeton University; Stanford Medical School; University of Chicago; University of Michigan Medical School; University of California at Berkeley; University of California at Los Angeles; York University, Canada; University of Edinburgh, Scotland; University of Lund, Sweden; University of Groningen, The Netherlands; University of New South Wales, Australia; Institut de la Rochefoucault, France; and National Institute of Industrial Health, Japan.

Studies have been published in many major scientific journals, including *Science, Lancet, Scientific American, American Journal of Physiology, International Journal of Neuroscience,*

Experimental Neurology, Electroencephalography and Clinical Neurophysiology, Psychosomatic Medicine, Journal of the Canadian Medical Association, American Psychologist, British Journal of Educational Psychology, Journal of Counseling Psychology, The Journal of Mind and Behavior, Academy of Management Journal, Journal of Conflict Resolution, Perceptual and Motor Skills, Criminal Justice and Behavior, Journal of Crime and Justice, Proceedings of the Endocrine Society, Journal of Clinical Psychiatry, and *Social Indicators Research.*

Many studies have been presented at professional scientific conferences, and others have been part of doctoral dissertations prepared under the guidance of thesis committees at leading universities. Much of the research has been gathered together in six volumes (over 5,000 pages) of scientific research on the Transcendental Meditation and the TM-Sidhi Programme, including Yogic Flying.

These studies have validated the profound benefits of the Transcendental Meditation Programme for the individual and for every area of society, including health, education, business, industry, rehabilitation, defence, agriculture, and government.

The following categories* of research findings document the benefits of regular practice of the Transcendental Meditation Programme for the individual in all fields of management, and the collective effect of the group practice of the TM-Sidhi Programme in business and industry. Included are the results of studies conducted in business and industrial settings as well as the results of other research of particular relevance to the field of management.

- Increased Organizational Ability.
- Optimizing Brain⁺ Functioning.
- Increased Intelligence and Creativity.
- Increased Clarity of Thinking and Perception.
- Increased Energy and Dynamism.
- Increased Efficiency.

---

* Refer to the original scientific papers reprinted in *Scientific Research on Maharishi's Transcendental Meditation and TM-Sidhi Programme, Collected Papers, Volumes 1–6* (over 5,000 pages).

⁺ This has been validated by scientific research on the functioning of the brain physiology of those practising

Continued on page 319 ...

- Increased Job Satisfaction.
- A Unique State of Deep Rest during Transcendental Meditation to Neutralize Stress Caused by Routine Work.
- Increased Freedom from Stress.
- Creating Unbounded Awareness to Neutralize the Boundaries Caused by Routine Work.
- Growth of Personal Integration and Fulfilment.
- Reduction in Negative Personality Characteristics.
- Improved Social Relationships.
- Growth of Perfect Health.
- Increased City, National, and International Prosperity through the *Maharishi Effect*.

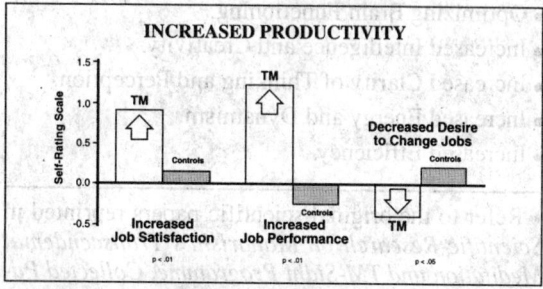

Subjects practising Maharishi's Transcendental Meditation Programme showed significant improvements at work with members of a control group. **Reference:** *Academy of Management Journal*, 17 (1974): 362–368.

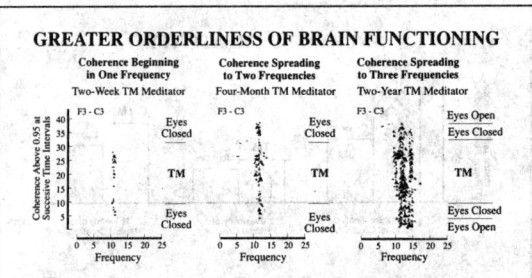

EEG coherence increases during the practice of the Transcendental Meditation Technique, indicating greater orderliness of brain functioning. **Reference:** *Psychosomatic Medicine*, 46 (1984); 267–276; *Proceedings of the San Diego Biomedical Symposium*, 15 (1976).

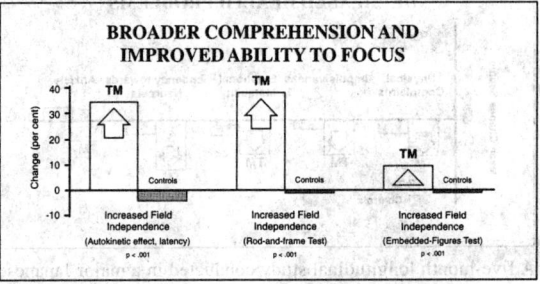

Students randomly assigned to learn Maharishi's Transcendental Meditation Technique displayed a significant increase over a three-month period, in comparison to controls, on three measures of field independence. Field independence indicates broader comprehension with increasing ability to focus. This systematic development of field independence in university students is unique.
Reference: *Perceptual and Motor Skills*, 39 (1974): 1031–1034.

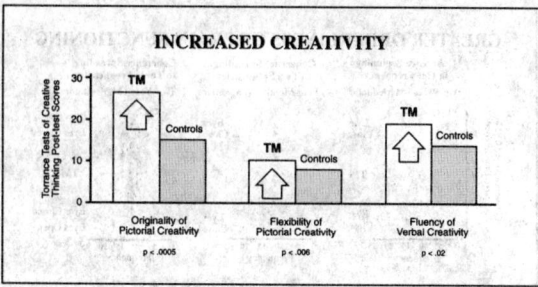

Students who learned Maharishi's Transcendental Meditation showed increased creativity over a five-month period. **Reference:** *The Journal of Creative Behavior,* 13 (1979): 169–180.

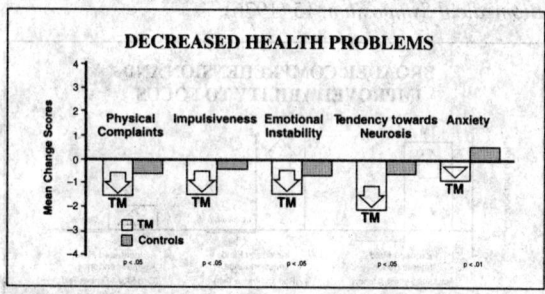

A five-month longitudinal study conducted in a major Japanese company, Simutomo Heavy Industries, by researchers from the National Institute of Industrial Health of the Japanese Ministry of Labour and the St. Marianna Medical Institute found significant improvements in physical and mental health in workers who practise the Transcendental Meditation Technique. **Reference:** *Japanese Journal of Industrial Health,* 32 (1990): 656; *Japanese Journal of Public Health,* 37 (1990): 729.

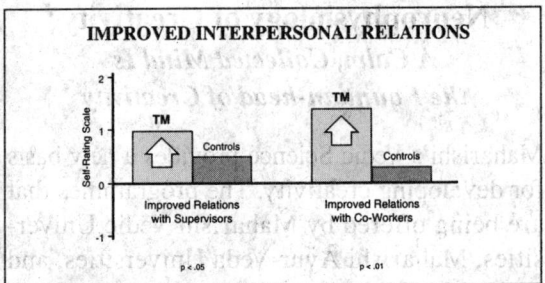

Both executives and employees experience better relations at work as a result of practising Maharishi's Transcendental Meditation, and the benefits increase over time. **Reference:** *Academy of Management Journal*, 17 (1974): 362–368.

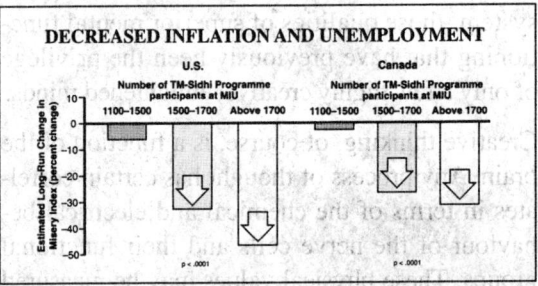

Time series analysis found a significant reduction in the economic 'misery index'—defined as the sum of the inflation rate and unemployment rate—when the number of participants in the group practice of the TM-Sidhi Programme exceeded the square root of one per cent of the North American population. **Reference:** *Proceedings of the Business and Economic Statistics Section, American Statistical Association*, (1987): 799–804; (1988): 491–496; (1989): 565–570.

Neurophysiology of Creativity
A Calm, Collected Mind Is the Fountain-head of Creativity

Maharishi's Vedic Science provides a new basis for developing creativity. The programmes that are being offered by Maharishi Vedic Universities, Maharishi Āyur-Veda Universities, and Maharishi Universities of Management will allow creativity to grow and flourish in every field of human activity. Everyone will instil in himself, on the level of the very cells of his nervous system, those qualities of superior[*] mental functioning that have previously been the privilege of only a few highly creative, enlightened minds.

Creative thinking, of course, is a function of the brain. Any process of thought has certain correlates in terms of the chemical and electrical behaviour of the nerve cells and their functional groups. These physical values may be measured and connected with their subjective correlates. For instance, the special type of thinking that is

---

[*] Refer to the research of Dr N. N. Lyubimov: Electrophysiological characteristics of mobilization of hidden

Continued on page 320 …

creative has associated with it certain physiological characteristics in the brain. What Transcendental Meditation does is to establish a pattern of orderly, coherent thinking and resistance to confusion at a direct neurophysiological level in the functioning of the brain, thereby facilitating creative thought.

To understand this, it is interesting to review what is known about the functioning of the different areas of the nervous system with respect to the mental capabilities that underlie creativity and to relate this information to laboratory measurements that have been used to verify the neurophysiological effects of Transcendental Meditation.

Two kinds of measurements have yielded especially dramatic and relevant results: electroencephalography, which measures the electrical activity of the cortex (the area of the brain that thinks), and galvanic skin response, which measures the overall stability of the nervous system, including emotional stability.

It has been shown that the EEG signals (brainwaves) induced during and after the practice of

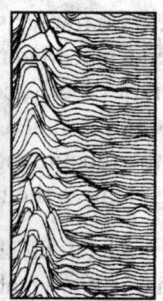

Computer-generated Fourier spectral analysis of electroencephalograph signals taken during Transcendental Meditation

Transcendental Meditation are remarkably synchronous and coherent and indicate superior integration and co-ordination of different brain areas. Three distinct types of integration are implied by this observed brainwave synchronization.

- First, brainwaves from the two cerebral hemispheres become purified in frequency and correlated in phase—they fall into step with one another. This finding has been replicated in many countries.

It was found that during Transcendental Meditation the energy output of the left and right hemispheres tends to become equalized, and the rhythmic activity from the two sides of the brain becomes statistically more*correlated, in phase, and*balanced.

Meditators also have more stable brain rhythms (8–12 Hertz), which are known to be correlated with reduced anxiety (anxiety inhibits creativity), improved psycho-technical performance, and the timing of voluntary actions (for creative behaviour). This increased stability of brain rhythms is believed to be the basis of the improved perceptual-motor performance that has been observed in meditators. Furthermore, there is evidence of increased activation of the right hemisphere after meditation and its correlated functions of intuition, spatial and melodic composition, and non-verbal idea formation—all important processes underlying creativity.

---

* Refer to scientific research: 'The Coherence Spectral Array (COSPAR) and Its Application to the Study of Spatial Ordering in the EEG', *Proceedings of the Continued on page 320* …

The increasing co-ordination of the activity of the two sides of the brain continues after meditation and accounts for the greater*creativity observed in meditators.

Creativity demands both intuition and a developed verbal and analytic capacity for the conception, formulation, communication and application of creative ideas in a simple and direct form. The increasing phase coherence between the activity of the two sides of the brain seen in meditators during and after Transcendental Meditation indicates functional integration of the intuitive, spatial skills of the right hemisphere with the analytic, verbal skills of the left hemisphere, indicating that Transcendental Meditation directly enlivens the neurophysiological basis of creativity.

- Second, brainwaves ordinarily characteristic of the posterior cortex (8-14 Hertz) spread synchronously and coherently to the frontal region to include the entire brain. Since the associa-

---

* Refer to scientific research: 'The TM Technique and Creativity: A Longitudinal Study of Cornell University Undergraduates', *The Journal of Creative Behavior*, 13 (1979): 169–180.

tion areas are in the anterior brain, the motor controls in the central regions, and the sensory processors throughout the brain, this profound ordering in terms of electrical wave synchrony has a suggested correlation with the improved co-ordination[*] of thought and action and improved perceptual-motor[+] performance experienced by meditators and evident in psychological tests. This provides a further basis for the expression of creativity in behaviour.

- The third type of electroencephalic ordering fundamental to creativity is seen in a more integrated relationship vertically, between the cortex and the thalamus and other subcortical centres.

This coherence between the parts of the brain responsible for conscious thinking (cortical) and for the primary physiological functions (subcortical) has the general consequence of

---

[*] Refer to scientific research: 'The Physiology of Meditation', *Scientific American*, 226 (1972): 84.

[+] Refer to scientific research: 'Effects of the Transcendental Meditation Technique on Normal and Jendrassik Reflex Time', *Perceptual and Motor Skills*, 50 (1980): 1103–1106.

a closer connection between mind and body and tends to elucidate the results of the now classical experiments, which showed that the purely mental technique of Transcendental Meditation had profound physiological effects producing deep relaxation to the entire system: reduced oxygen consumption, reduced metabolic rate, reduced breath rate, reduced cardiac output, increased skin resistance, and a decrease in blood lactate—a physiological index of reduced*anxiety.

It is common knowledge that a relaxed individual, free from the distractions of anxiety and worry, can more easily and more completely apply his creative potential.

It is also important to emphasize the cumulative nature of the benefits of the twice-daily practice of Transcendental Meditation and the TM-Sidhi Programme, and it is striking to no-

---

* Refer to scientific research: 'Differential Effects of Relaxation Techniques on Trait Anxiety: a Meta-Analysis', *Journal of Clinical Psychology*, 45 (1989): 957–974; and 'The Effect of the Transcendental Meditation Technique on Anxiety Level', *Journal of Clinical Psychology*, 33 (1977): 1076–1078.

tice that in every major study, the beneficial psychological and physiological effects of Transcendental Meditation have been found to increase without significant leveling off as the practice is continued.

Improved Brain Function—
Skill in Activity

The improvements in brain function deduced from measurements of EEG synchrony suggest integration of synthetic and analytic thinking, better linguistic and verbal ability, a widened range of idea associations, better mind-body co-ordination and more effortless memory, the hallmarks of a creative individual. Moreover, Transcendental Meditation has succeeded in establishing these qualities not on the level of reasoning or psychology alone, but directly and deeply at the level of the neurophysiological structure of the brain. Thus Transcendental Meditation makes the habit of creative thinking spontaneous in the individual.

---

* Refer to scientific research: 'A Wakeful Hypometabolic Physiologic State', *American Journal of*
Continued on page 321 ...

Daily practice of Transcendental Meditation quickly renders clarity and liveliness normal features of brain functioning and therefore creativity a normal feature of any undertaking.

Another aspect of creative thinking is the power to resist disorganization due to environmental changes. The maintenance of orderliness through the stability and adaptability of the thinking process provides individuals with freedom from confusion in the midst of external disorderly influences.

This quality of resistance to disorientation has also been shown objectively to be generated by the practice of Transcendental Meditation. The experiments on galvanic skin response show that meditators respond much more stably to a stressful (disorderly) stimulus than non-meditators and recover more quickly with less retention of disorientation—a direct and accepted measure of emotional balance and strength. In addition, direct measures of emotional health by standard

---

* Refer to scientific research: 'Autonomic Stability and Transcendental Meditation', *Psychosomatic Continued on page 322 …*

tests of psychological functioning clearly reveal that meditators grow in the values of self-actualization, firm identity, spontaneity, and solidity of character—qualities which can only promote the free and full expression of creative intelligence.

To summarize, Transcendental Meditation is seen to be a quite natural and easily learned mental technique that immediately generates a coherent and orderly pattern of functioning in the groups of neurons which compose the brain, and this is reflected in synchronous electrical activity, which seems to be correlated with observed improvements in many aspects of the functioning of creativity in meditators. Taking this information together, it is not surprising that research has shown a significant increase in the rate of growth*of intelligence (I.Q.) in a group of meditators compared to a control group. From these results of improved brain functioning, increased intelligence, increased stability in the

---

* Refer to scientific research: 'Consciousness and Cognitive Development: A Six-Month Longitudinal Study of Four-Year-Olds Practicing the Children's
Continued on page 322 …

face of stress, solidity of character and increased spontaneity, it is clear that Transcendental Meditation is fundamental to the development of a high level of creativity.

Deep Rest and Increasing Order— the Third Law of Thermodynamics: an Analogy from Physical Science

It is obvious that creativity is interdependent with the value of orderliness. This interdependence of creativity with increasing orderliness leads us to inquire more deeply into the natural laws which govern order.

Therefore it is important that the entire pattern of increased orderliness of thought through Transcendental Meditation, established on the level of neurophysiology, may be understood from an even more general scientific standpoint. The deep order of the brain and mind during Transcendental Meditation is correlated with the deep rest—inactivity—that is produced by this technique, exemplified by a metabolic rate lower than the lowest rate established in deep sleep. This rule of 'creative intelligence through rest' seems to be analogous to a very general Law of Nature discovered by the science of Physics to apply to all natural systems.

This law, the Third Law of Thermodynamics, states that entropy (disorder) decreases when temperature (activity) decreases and that the condition of zero entropy, perfect orderliness, coin-

Subjectively Thinking Becomes More Orderly

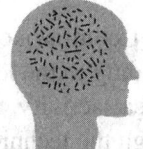 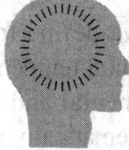

Thought is disorderly in the absence of pure consciousness

Transcendental Meditation establishes the field of pure consciousness

After Transcendental Meditation thought retains orderliness

When the source of thought is enlivened, all the impulses of the mind align themselves with the field of creative intelligence. This explains why the thinking of the meditator becomes spontaneously evolutionary. Single impulses of thought representing components of individual intelligence align themselves with the field of Cosmic Intelligence once that unbounded area of intelligence has been enlivened by the contact of individual intelligence.

cides with a temperature of absolute zero (absolutely no activity). In fact, the region near absolute zero temperature in physical systems is closely connected with a strong tendency towards wave coherence and synchrony and is exemplified in the onset of superfluidity and superconductivity near absolute zero temperature when activity is minimum. This suggests a striking analogy to the synchrony of brainwaves induced by the very deep rest of Transcendental Meditation.

If we define for the purpose of comparison a 'mental temperature', corresponding to the level of mental and neurophysiological activity, and systematically reduce this through the technique of Transcendental Meditation, we perceive a class of tendencies in the human mind that reminds us of the Third Law of Thermodynamics as seen in the realm of basic Physics. This quantum-mechanical analogy suggests that orderliness in the brain and in thinking is natural to man. Transcendental Meditation accomplishes this orderliness by providing an opportunity for the mind to follow the natural tendency of the most general patterns of Nature. The source of creativity is therefore the regime of reduced 'mental temperature'.

This natural tendency towards orderliness is the 'natural evolutionary impulse of life'. The physicist Schrödinger found that the orderly, creative (low entropy) aspect of life was closely tied to the order-preserving quality of the quantum-mechanical nature of the DNA molecule, a quality characteristic of the region near absolute zero temperature. He found further that all life depended, for a continuing state of creative order and an avoidance of the disorganization of death, upon the ability to 'drink orderliness from the environment'.

We may interpret the process of Transcendental Meditation as a specifically human means of 'drinking orderliness' by a purely mental process. This technique does indeed result in a synchronous brainwave pattern of markedly lower

---

* The Vedic Expression for this is:

भद्रं कर्णेभिः शृणुयाम देवा भद्रं पश्येमाक्षभिर्यजत्राः

*Bhadraṁ karṇebhiḥ shriṇuyām Devā
bhadraṁ pashyemā kshabhir-yajatrāḥ* ...

(Ṛk Veda, 1.89.8)

entropy. From this view, Transcendental Meditation can be seen as something absolutely basic and simple that runs parallel to and communicates with the simplest features of universal physical laws. The source of creativity tapped by Transcendental Meditation is the same source as for all of the Laws of Nature.

Innovative Thinking—Channeling Creativity for Accomplishment

There is one more element important to the mental life of each individual. Just as orderly thinking is not useful without lively creativity, so creativity and inventiveness are not useful without a habit of orderliness. It is orderly thinking that provides a productive and useful direction for imagination.

Inventiveness will only find its goal if it remains active, progressive, and evolutionary—well-guided, channeled, and defined—so that creativity takes a straight line from its source in the pure liveliness of the mind to its goal in achievement through practical activity.

The degree of a man's creativity has thus far

proved to be inaccessible to meaningful objective measurement, but it is clear that creativity must depend on the ability of the nervous system to provide a wide range of idea-associations with a speed and facility of mental response, both of which are strongly implied by the type of EEG synchrony observed in meditators.

The individual who meditates finds his mind simultaneously more creative, more clear, and more lucid, and his channel of progress in any field of activity becomes smoother and more direct. This is established deep in the physiological structure of the brain.

Creativity in Management Training

Subjectively, students who begin Transcendental Meditation report that academic work becomes easier and more enjoyable. They are more productive while spending the same amount of time at work, their level of interest and motivation is higher and more consistent, career goals spontaneously become better defined, and their experience of education in general becomes increasingly more rewarding and successful.

Clearly all these benefits to the activity of study, well documented by laboratory experiments, make Transcendental Meditation the most valuable element of educational technology ever offered to the world's educational systems.

Transcendental Meditation can accomplish directly the clear style of thinking that in the past was the result of heredity or else the fruit of years of disciplined training. The stability and clarity which previously belonged only to mature people with a lifetime of learning can now be given directly to young students.

Students who have dropped out of school find that after starting Transcendental Meditation they spontaneously gain the desire to return, since by making knowledge easier to acquire, Transcendental Meditation renders it more fascinating and attractive.

Furthermore, the very complex and integrated function of the brain called motivation is enhanced by Transcendental Meditation. This capacity is most certainly not available through any other known means which is so adaptable to a wide variety of cultures, traditions, and life styles.

Naturally, students experiencing the great advantage of orderly thinking that comes about through the practice of Maharishi's Vedic Science will want to intellectually understand what is happening as well. For this reason, Maharishi University of Management is designing programmes in Maharishi's Master Management, both theory and practice, to be available to every school and college.

For all of the reasons described above, Transcendental Meditation must be included as a normal part of management training at every level of education. It is just these benefits of the knowledge and practice of Maharishi's Vedic Science that has inspired Maharishi University of Management to make Maharishi's Master Management universally available to students in all institutions of management, so that the youth of every generation may be prepared to effectively meet the challenge of the fast pace of progress in the modern world of science and technology.

Maharishi's Master Management and Job Satisfaction in Business, Industry, and Civil Service

- **The Problem:** *Boredom and Routine Activity*

In many of the professions in society, especially those of factory workers and civil service employees, to become truly expert on the job requires a strict focusing of vision and action to the narrow boundaries of a particular and routine task.

The effect of a repetitious, rigid routine and highly specialized daily activity is to develop in the worker a style of thinking within boundaries that quickly loses freshness and broad perspective. Moreover, this habit of remaining within boundaries and its resultant way of thinking carry over considerably into family and social life. Thus the population is prevented from expressing that judgement, insight, and integrity which are man's birthright and which are spontaneously available through natural, daily contact with the field of pure Creative Intelligence.

In some experiments this vicious circle of narrowing perception due to routine work has been partially or temporarily overcome. When theoretical knowledge of the nature, social significance, and ultimate purpose of the job is given to the worker, his appreciation and understanding tend to expand beyond the mundane boundaries of his daily task. Another attempt at transcending boundaries has been the moving of labourers from one operation to another. Although retraining is required with each move, changing jobs often stimulates the needed creative overview.

In both cases, the principle was right—increased perspective and freshness of vision are necessary to free the workers from remaining bogged down in the boundaries of routine behaviour—but in practice it proved time-consuming and only temporarily effective.

● *The Solution: Permanently Expand Vision through Maharishi's Vedic Science and Technology of Consciousness—Maharishi's Master Management*

The logical extension of this principle—expand awareness to overcome the boundaries created by routine and repetitious activity—is to take away permanently all boundaries that restrict the spontaneous, unlimited appreciation of life. By regularly contacting the inner field of unbounded awareness, or pure consciousness, through Transcendental Meditation, every working man naturally experiences a greatly expanded awareness. He increasingly sustains an unbounded overview of all his thought and action from the perspective of that unchanging, boundless field of pure intelligence which is his own inner life.

Through Maharishi's Master Management the addition of theoretical knowledge about this universal basis of life, pure intelligence, augments the experience of widening awareness and diminishing boundaries by providing a systematic understanding of the processes involved. Life is shown to develop and evolve in a consistent and rational way, and since this new appreciation of the evolutionary nature of life is relevant to all human activity, every worker comes to regard his daily routine as simply the outer means of stabilizing his accelerating enjoyment of life as a whole.

025

Maharishi's Vedic Management
The Complete Science and Technology of Management

Maharishi University of Management is in possession of that complete science and technology of management, which commands and controls the future (Maharishi Jyotish); which unifies all diversifying tendencies (Maharishi Yoga); maintaining a healthy, nourishing environment, where everything supports everything else—where Cosmic Creative Intelligence upholds individual creativity (Maharishi Sthāpathya Veda); enlivening harmony, WHOLENESS, and Unity in everything that is separate from everything else (Maharishi Gandharva Veda); promoting balance, continuity, longevity, and vitality in the field of change—promoting health and WHOLENESS in the natural flow of evolution (Maharishi Āyur-Veda); and upholding the infinite speed of dynamism on the ground of eternal silence—maintaining the lively presence of the goal at every step of the path—achieving the goal at every step of the

---

* Total one-pointed focus on the target—the com-
Continued ...

path—the skill of irresistibly attracting the goal rather than proceeding on the path to it—the pathless path of management through the Principle of Least Action—the absolute system of management without stress and strain that achieves the goal in minimum time (Maharishi Dhanur-Veda).

• Without the ability to control the future it is not possible for any management to be really stable, successful, and continuously rewarding. That is why Maharishi Jyotish is an essential characteristic feature of my Vedic Management—Maharishi's Vedic Management.

The perfection of the 'Science of Time' (Maharishi Jyotish) lies not only in identifying events in the future, but more importantly, it has the technology to change any future into a brighter future. Without the ability to command the fu-

---

Footnote continues ...
pletely natural, simplest state of awareness projecting a desire from the infinitely correlated level of awareness, the level of pure life that is fully free from obstacles, which in its absolute freedom promotes bubbling bliss—the frictionless flow of desire—finding the target at the source of the path.

ture, management will always be a football of situations and circumstances.

• Without the ability to maintain a unifying influence in the diversifying ever-evolving values, no administrator can ever succeed in maintaining an integrated, progressive society, and no management can ever maintain a coherent, healthy, happy environment. That is why the element of Maharishi Yoga is an absolute requirement for the stability, integrity, and progress of any management.

• Without the ability to maintain the connectedness of any one specific area of management with all other areas of management and also with the holistic area of management, no administration or management can be fulfilling to itself or to its purpose. That is why Maharishi Sthāpatya Veda is an absolute requirement of any management.

• Without the ability to maintain harmony—a nourishing influence within individuals and within their environment—no administration or management can sustain continued success. That is why Maharishi Gandharva Veda is an essential element in the field of management.

- Without the ability to maintain balance—good health—no administration or management can breathe life. Maharishi Āyur-Veda brings health, vitality, and creativity to the field of Management.

- Without the ability to focus sharply while maintaining broad comprehension, no management can successfully fulfil its purpose. Maharishi Dhanur-Veda, offering the field of infinite correlation, makes management invincible, and is therefore an absolute requirement for sustained success in every field of management.

Endowed with the enormous potential of these few above-mentioned values, Maharishi's Vedic Management has custody of the absolute efficiency of management.

In this way it is easy to appreciate that all the thirty-seven* qualities of Natural Law, the thirty-seven values of Maharishi's Vedic Management, have to be an integral part of any management.

It is very important for every individual to un-

---

* Refer to pages 26–29.

derstand the significance of Maharishi Jyotish, Maharishi Yoga, Maharishi Sthāpatya Veda, and all the other thirty-seven values of Natural Law, as available in the Vedic Literature, and as expressed in the human physiology.

To understand the infinite diversity of the wholeness of Natural Law spread over the whole universe, and to understand the connection of individual life with Cosmic Life it is necessary for everyone to know that every part of everyone's physiology has a counterpart in the physiology of the cosmos.

For this it is necessary to study the following illustrations (pages 230–232) with reference to the value of Maharishi Āyur-Veda, Maharishi Jyotish, Maharishi Sthāpatya Veda, and Maharishi Yoga, which connect the reality* of the structure and function of the individual with the reality* of the structure and function of the whole cosmos.

No individual, organization, or nation can live

Continued on page 233 ...

---

* This is no surprise to anyone who understands the cosmic spread of the Unified Field of Natural Law (Quantum Physics), and the 'wave function of the universe' (Quantum Cosmology).

Influence from all over the Universe on the Earth and the Human Brain
The Counterpart of the Individual Physiology Discovered in the Cosmic Physiology of the Universe

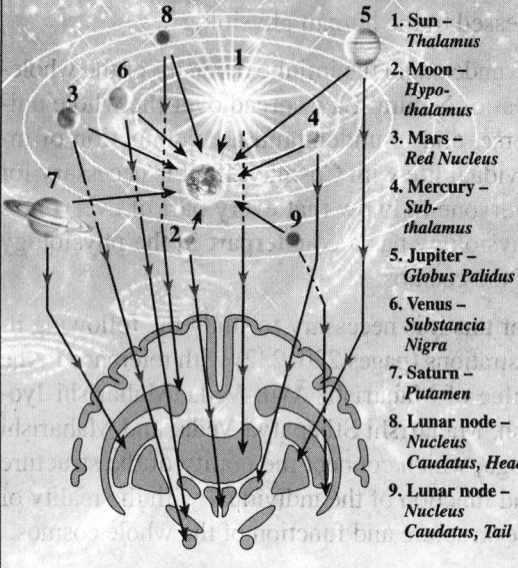

1. Sun – *Thalamus*
2. Moon – *Hypothalamus*
3. Mars – *Red Nucleus*
4. Mercury – *Subthalamus*
5. Jupiter – *Globus Palidus*
6. Venus – *Substancia Nigra*
7. Saturn – *Putamen*
8. Lunar node – *Nucleus Caudatus, Head*
9. Lunar node – *Nucleus Caudatus, Tail*

This picture shows a coronal section of the brain with its internal structures and their one-to-one relation to the planets. Perfect order and balance in the structure and function of the universe is reflected in the structure and function of the human physiology.

(For simplicity, only a few of the aspects of the comprehensive connections between the universe and the physiology are shown in this illustration.)

Influence from all over the Universe on the Earth and the Human Brain
The Counterpart of the Individual Physiology Discovered in the Cosmic Physiology of the Universe

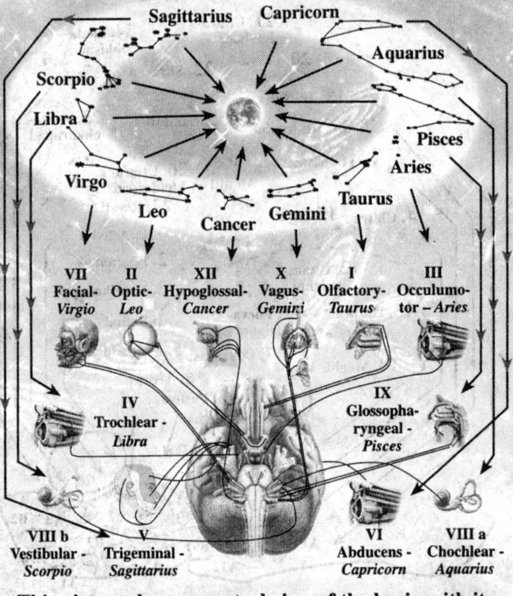

- Sagittarius
- Capricorn
- Aquarius
- Scorpio
- Libra
- Pisces
- Aries
- Virgo
- Leo
- Cancer
- Gemini
- Taurus

VII Facial - *Virgio*
II Optic - *Leo*
XII Hypoglossal - *Cancer*
X Vagus - *Gemini*
I Olfactory - *Taurus*
III Occulumotor – *Aries*
IV Trochlear - *Libra*
IX Glossopharyngeal - *Pisces*
VIII b Vestibular - *Scorpio*
V Trigeminal - *Sagittarius*
VI Abducens - *Capricorn*
VIII a Chochlear - *Aquarius*

This picture shows a ventral view of the brain with its 12 cranial nerves and their one-to-one relation to the constellations. Perfect order and balance in the structure and function of the universe is reflected in the structure and function of the human physiology.

(For simplicity, only a few of the aspects of the comprehensive connections between the universe and the physiology are shown in this illustration.)

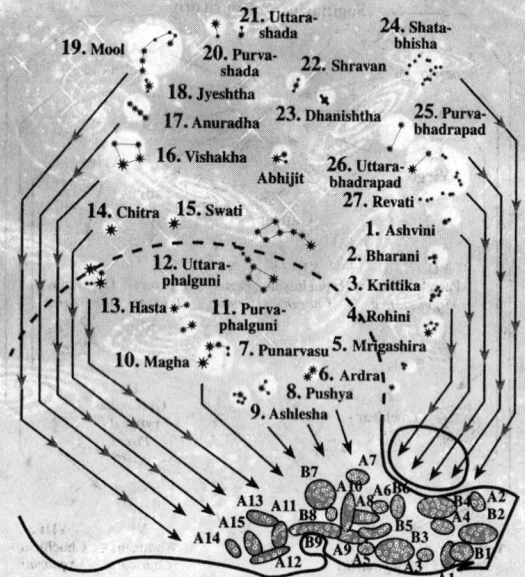

Influence from all over the Universe on the Earth and the Human Brain

The Counterpart of the Individual Physiology Discovered in the Cosmic Physiology of the Universe

This picture shows a sagittal section of the brain stem with its internal structures and their one-to-one relation to collections of distant stars. Perfect order and balance in the structure and function of the universe is reflected in the structure and function of the human physiology.

(For simplicity, only 14 of the 27 connections are shown here.)

an integrated life unless their individual identity on earth is fully integrated with the cosmic identity of the universe—no individual, organization, or nation can live up to their full potential unless they are in full alliance with Cosmic Life.

For centuries, and even we can say for ages, this knowledge of Natural Law which connects the life of the individual with Cosmic Life was not practically available. Now it has been brought to light and its significance has been validated through scientific research and through direct experience.

Now is the time to rejoice in the sunshine of a great new fortune—the complete knowledge of Natural Law, which is available for everyone to enjoy.

It is the unimaginable great fortune of mankind that this perfect system of management—holistic management through Natural Law—Vedic Management—has been made practical.

Maharishi's Vedic Management has authority in this royal theme of management, which enjoys freedom on the ground of its ability to spontaneously turn around any situation or circumstance in favour of success.

> Every individual in authority in any field of management, whether he manages a small industry or holds the reins of the enormous power in the administration of a big government, should take notice of the fact that any system of management or system of administration must be endowed with the ability to utilize all the thirty-seven qualities of intelligence, including their divisions and subdivisions, as available in Maharishi's Vedic Management—Maharishi's Master Management, which is Absolute Management, endowed with the infinite organizing power of Natural Law.

No individual can be successful in any field unless his system of management is endowed with each of the thirty-seven values of management, separately and collectively.

---

* It is these thirty-seven qualities of intelligence that present one holistic value of Natural Law in Ṛk Veda

Continued on page 323 ...

No individual can be a successful manager unless he is trained in the ability to spontaneously utilize all the thirty-seven areas of creativity and their divisions and subdivisions that together constitute the infinite organizing power of Natural Law; no management can be really successful unless the thirty-seven values of creativity are lively in the simplest state of the manager's awareness.

Maharishi's Vedic Management enlivens all the thirty-seven values of the organizing power of Natural Law—the thirty-seven qualities of management—in the simplest state of the manager's awareness, giving him the custody of the holistic value of Natural Law, which renders management simple, thorough, effective, and fulfilling.

The only royal* way to perfection is through my Natural Law-Based Management—Maharishi's Master Management.

---

* Thirty years ago a wave of emotion swelled up and voiced:

I am the way to Thee, my Lord,
Thou art the goal in me.

The same feeling swells up now when I am saying:
Continued on page 323 …

Cry for Help

USA TODAY, 21 December 1994, documents the rise of stress in top level management in its article: 'Harvard president to return after medical leave'.

Maharishi University of Management is going to eliminate the problems of stress in all fields of management by introducing the all-directional performance of the infinite organizing power of Natural Law in the intelligence of the manager.

In an article 'Business Schools' Formula for Irrelevance', *Wall Street Journal*, 28 November 1994, a lawyer, who teaches law and business ethics in a college of business, with 17 years of teaching experience (six deans, and four curriculum revisions), concludes that much of business education is overly quantitative and far removed from actual business practice. He addresses the oft-asked question: What's wrong with business schools and business education?

> *An answer obvious to an insider is that what many of my colleagues are teach-*

ing to both graduates and undergraduates is essentially irrelevant and unusable in business. ...

... Our students need the skills to solve unstructured problems, well beyond the journal equations. Analytical skills require more than just model design. We train our students as quantitative dweebs and then puzzle as to why businesses are hiring liberal-arts majors. ...

... What we research and teach in business schools is so far removed from what businesses do that even our MBA students sell back their textbooks.

Our students need the basics of marketing, finance, management, economics, and information systems. They need communication and interpersonal skills. They need law with a strong understanding of ethical values. They are not getting what they need.

In another article 'College Courses on Accounting Get Poor Grade', the *Wall Street Journal*, 12 August 1994, concludes that college accounting courses do not sufficiently teach students the accounting skills most needed for effectiveness in business.

> Business leaders feel current college accounting courses don't sufficiently teach students the skills they really need to be effective in business, according to a major report by a six-member joint committee of the 85,000-member Institute of Management Accountants and the 14,000-member Financial Executives Institute.
>
> The report 'attacks the entire fabric of accounting education', some panel members say. ...
>
> ... Even the American Assembly of Collegiate Schools of Business, whose members include 675 such schools in the U.S.A., concedes that accounting courses poorly prepare students for jobs in business. ... 'But we can't move mountains', says Jane Rubin, the AACSB's director of accounting accreditation. It will take years, if not decades,

> *for the nation's business schools to come around to meeting businesses' needs.'*

And regarding the proposal for 150 hours of accounting education for accounting majors to be offered in U.S. colleges, associate dean of the University of Alabama's School of Business and president of the management accountants institute is quoted as saying that the 150-hour programme is:

> *'useless unless it teaches students how to make*key business decisions in cost accounting, budgeting, and business strategies.'*

An article by the Dean of the business school at Indiana University, 'Nothing Succeeds Like Training for Success', *Wall Street Journal*, 12 September 1994, identifies the characteristics

---

* The key to making strategic decisions is to unlock the door that segregates the holistic value of management from the individual values of managerial concern.

Management has to be in a progressive sequence, but
Continued on page 324 ...

of highly successful companies and challenges management schools to teach their students these principles of success:

> *Training people to succeed requires that they develop an integrated view from the beginning; they must think of business as a strategic whole, not as a collection of disciplines joined loosely at the top. Executives also must be taught to communicate effectively, since the most sophisticated vision is of no use unless it can be clearly understood by others.*

Examining high performing companies that provide world-class training, he observes:

> *This concentration on developing world-class skills means business must keep up with the rapid evolution in the real world. Extensive links between schools and companies must be built to ensure that research and teaching has relevance as well as intellectual integrity.*

And looking at high-performing companies which value 'people skills':

> *Top management must constantly monitor whether its stars are being used and developed to their potential. At the same time, executives must be sure that performance problems are not covered up. For management schools, this means that effective interpersonal skills are at least as critical as accounting acumen....*

Finally, noting that high-performing companies are entrepreneurial:

> *When banks lend money to big companies, they focus on financial and industry analyses and typically have a terrible record in predicting problems. But as a bank lending mostly to small companies, my bank knew that the strength and intensity of the leaders, their understanding of their business, the reliability of their structures, and the depth of their talent were the real predictors of long-term success. The bank examiners hated these kinds of loans because it was hard to document these factors. But we slept better when*

they were present.

He concludes:

The challenge for our management schools is to teach this 'success mindset' so it permeates the next generation of corporate leaders.

Maharishi University of Management aligns the consciousness of the manager with the evolutionary direction of Natural Law and thereby fulfils the demand of teaching the 'success mindset'—mind set on success—mind spontaneously, without stress and strain, set in the evolutionary direction (of Natural Law).

It is fortunate that the world of management has realized the need for something that can eliminate the weakness of management and provide a better and fuller education and training in the field of management.

Credit goes to those recognized leaders of management in the world today who have pin-pointed the weak areas of management training, and have indicated the need for improvement.

World-wide dissatisfaction of education and training in management has really helped to hasten the process of the development of a new, complete theme of management. A complete science and art of management has been fully developed and is being made available to all through Maharishi University of Management.

Successful Founders of Family Industries

There is a need for the preservation and constant revitalization of the original creativity of the successful founders of family industries.

The history of the decline of the original brilliance of family industries is due to lack of proper management training, which, focusing basically on economics, shadows the managing intelligence of Nature—the Creative Intelligence in any individual—and hampers the free and full expression of the evolutionary quality of consciousness.

Not enough emphasis on the element of consciousness, the managing intelligence of each individual, results in the decline of health and creativity: a flower without water naturally fades.

India Business Intelligence (newsletter of the FINANCIAL TIMES), 2 November 1994, in its article 'Why some Indian business families are in decline' reports:

> *The old order changeth. A recent survey of Indian business families shows that many of the most eminent names of a couple of decades ago are no longer at the top of the totem-pole. Among the drop-outs are the Bangurs, the Kirloskars, the Modis, the Scindias, the Sarabhais, and ICI.*
>
> *Some, like ICI and the Scindias, were victims of muddled management. These factors, and the lethargy evident in older groups, did play their part in the decline of business families. But the most important reason remains the tendency to fission given the slightest chance. Most groups*

when they reach the third generation have been carved up by the various family factions; even the Birlas had to go through such a division. In the west, by the time the third generation comes along, ownership gets divorced from management. In India, unfortunately, that does not happen. The third generation, with none of the talents of their entrepreneur grandfather, allow their companies to quickly go to seed.

More interesting than looking at the dismal failures are the success stories. In 1976, the Ambanis of Reliance were a lowly 67th. Today, they not only preside over India's largest private sector company, they occupy the third spot as a group (after the Tatas and the BK-Aditya Birla combine). The Ruias (now No 4) were not even ranked in the earlier survey. R.P. Goenka (now No 6) was 60th.

These success stories have been well documented. Not so well known, perhaps, are the likely candidates on the top-20 list a decade down the line. While this can only be a matter of conjecture, some indus-

> *trialists stand out because of the track-scorching pace they have set. Among them are the Dhoots of Videocon, the Nambiars of BPL, the Mehtas of Torrent, the Handas of Core Parenterals, the Lohias of Indo-Rama, the O.P. Jindals, the Sanghis, the Parasrampurias ....*
>
> *The rise and fall of business families is of course as inevitable as the seasons. Fortunately for the rest of us, few of them are able to establish dynasties. One can be certain that many of today's leading names will vanish from tomorrow's league tables.*

Maharishi University of Management has been established to save all companies and corporations in the world from decline.

Through the programmes of Maharishi University of Management there is no need for any rising industry today to be the falling industry of tomorrow. Now there is no reason why the original brilliance exemplified by the founder of any successful family company or any other company should fade over generations.

A small percentage of profit spent on the welfare of the company—to maintain the health, vitality, and creativity of the company—will go a long way to ensure the ever-progressive performance and success of the company.

Maharishi University of Management will maintain the vitality of the company by aligning the managing intelligence of the company with the ever-progressive, ever-evolutionary managing intelligence of Nature, ensuring that the company always continues to progress on the waves of success.

Through the programmes of Maharishi University of Management, the personnel department of the company will maintain good health, vitality, and creativity; the employer-employee relationship will be fulfilling to all, and the company will maintain progress without stress.

The emphasis that is laid on the programmes of Maharishi University of Management has its basis in my reinterpretation and revival of Vedic Knowledge, and research in the field of consciousness, which is the most basic element of life, from where all areas of life are administered.

248

Everything depends on the quality of management. Maharishi University of Management trains the manager to achieve rising levels of economy without allowing stress, strain, and problems to overshadow the life of anyone involved in the company.

Turn Around

Maharishi's Master Management turns around all the problems of management by developing **full alertness, full creativity,** and **full support of Nature** through proper education and training, achieving the immediate and distant goals of management.

Full alertness, full creativity, and **full support of Nature** results from:

1. Release of stress;
2. Increased vitality;
3. Improved health;
4. Nourishing working environment.

Full alertness, full creativity, and **full support of Nature** results in:

1. Increased production and sales;
2. A healthy level of competitiveness maintained in national and international markets;
3. Improved health, wealth, and wisdom of each individual and the company as a whole;
4. Ever-increasing success and fulfilment of the company, day by day.

Maharishi's Master Management offers preven-

tion and also cure—it prevents failures, disallows problems, and promotes progress and increasing success.

The absolute formula for perfect management is to open our awareness to the infinite organizing power of Natural Law, which is the manager within our own body.* Opening our awareness to the infinite organizing power of Natural Law means opening our awareness to the managing intelligence of Natural Law,+ which is the total potential of Natural Law.

When our awareness is open to this level of intelligence within ourself then the organizing power of Natural Law is spontaneously awake in our intellect, mind, senses, and behaviour, and all our thought, speech, and action spontaneously flows in the evolutionary direction of Natural Law.

The formula to gain mastery over management

---

* Refer to 'Natural Law, Cosmic Manager of the Universe, Invincible Source of Order and Harmony Discovered in the Human Physiology', pages 123–169.

+ Refer to 'Managing Intelligence of Nature', page 19.

is to gain custody of this infinite organizing power of Natural Law in our awareness, for which the call of Natural Law from within everyone is 'return—come back*' and be established in self-referral consciousness, and inspire the infinite organizing power of Natural Law to work⁺ for you.

The same call comes from the Bhagavad-Gītā, one of the textbooks of Natural Law, which is also reverberating in the inner intelligence of the body of everyone:

निस्त्रैगुरायो भवार्जुन

Nistrai-guṇyo bhav-Arjuna
(Bhagavad-Gītā, 2.45)
Be without the three Guṇas, O Arjuna!

The Bhagavad-Gītā sings the song of invincibility; it sings the song of the absolute managing power eternally lively, eternally functioning,

---

* *Nivartadhwam* (Ṛk Veda, 10.19.1).

⁺ *Brahmā bhavati sārathiḥ* (Ṛk Veda, 1.158.6).

⊕ The Itihas is one of the thirty-six values of the Vedic Literature, which in its physiological form is expressed in the voluntary motor and sensory projections.

eternally managing the eternally complex diversity of our physiology.

It is only necessary that our awareness does not remain closed to it. Our awareness should remain open to it. Whatever our awareness will open to will be served by the infinite organizing power of our own self-referral managing intelligence. This means that the development of managerial skills should primarily centre in gaining the self-referral state of intelligence, and only secondary importance should be given to gathering information about different values of one's concern or one's profession.

The structure of Veda—the structuring dynamics of the inner intelligence of our body—is the basic field of infinite organizing power, which is simultaneously and constantly engaged in managing the innumerable diverse functions of the physiology. This is that level of the perfect skill of management, which manages*innumerable diverse values simultaneously.

---

* Even one thought stimulates the holistic value and all the innumerable values of the physiology. Even
Continued on page 325 ...

The discovery of the thirty-seven areas of the physiology, the dynamics of the managing power of intelligence structured in thirty-seven qualities of the self-referral field of intelligence, has given us the lively manager, active manager, functioning manager, within everyone.

Training in managerial skills requires opening our awareness to this level of intelligence, which just amounts to gaining familiarity with the lively field of managing intelligence.

Maharishi University of Management has been established[*] for everyone to gain familiarity with this central switchboard of Cosmic Management, which is already the functioning intelligence of everyone's body.

The goal is to open this inner treasury to everyone, on all levels of thought, speech, and action.

Due to lack of knowledge about this theme of developing excellence in management, the whole field of management is full of problems.

Maharishi University of Management handles

---

[*] May 1995.

the turn around of any company or the restoration of any failing industry from this field of managing intelligence, which is lively within everyone. In the case of a company, the turn around will only be complete on a permanent basis when everyone in the company has the opportunity to avail of this holistic management, this complete theme of training in management, so that they handle every aspect of their life successfully.

There is a common proverb that 'there are wheels within wheels', and the gearbox of management has to be so organized that each wheel contributes to the smooth running of every other wheel. This secret of management, practised in Maharishi's Master Management, places management on a level of that efficiency and effectiveness of Natural Law, which governs the universe with perfect order and eternally in a problem-free manner.

This aspect of 'wheels within wheels' is displayed in the hierarchy of the absolute management of Natural Law. This hierarchy has one eternal Unity on the top—self-referral consciousness—and gains the structure of Law, Natural Law, when it is expressed as Saṁhitā of Ṛishi, Devatā, Chhandas—the unified state of three structures, or three qualities, of Ṛishi, Devatā, Chhandas, or the observer, process of observation, and the observed—total subjectivity, objectivity, and their relationship.

This second stage of the hierarchy of management sequentially evolves into major clusters of three, nine, twelve, twenty-seven, and thirty-seven, and each of these clusters have their own divisions and subdivisions, and the divisions and subdivisions of each of these clusters have their perfect theory and its application for the alignment of any management with the perfect management of Natural Law.

Study of these areas of excellence in management constitute the mainstream of training in Maharishi University of Management. This training develops the ability to prevent problems and to achieve 'company turn around' for any company, big or small.

To gain mastery in management (real first class

MBA) will take some time, but the ability to use a few formulas from all these thirty-six clusters of the organizing power of Natural Law does not take much time. It can be likened to building a machine, which requires a much longer time than learning how to operate it.

This is the first generation to offer solutions to the problems of management in the thousands of years of struggling history of management; that is why, due to lack of the availability of a sufficiently large number of trained experts, Maharishi University of Management will be accepting just a few cases of 'company turn around' during 1995, which is going to be the first year to introduce perfection in the field of management for centuries to come—for all ages to come.

We are using the phrase 'for ages to come' because of the perfection of this system of training in management through Natural Law. There

---

* As Maharishi University of Management is being established in many parts of the world, very soon there will be an adequate number of trained experts to put an end to all problems of management.

can be no improvement to the offer of Maharishi's Master Management, which is completely competent to meet the requirements of management for all times. There can be no improvement to the efficiency and effectiveness of management through Natural Law—nothing can ever supercede Maharishi's Master Management in the whole range of performance of Natural Law for all future times.

This claim is being made on the ground of the absolute precision of my Vedic Mathematics, which is the Mathematics of the Absolute Number.

The Absolute Number has provided the mathematics (system of unfailing precision) of the relationship between the absolute, holistic value of Natural Law and specific values of Natural Law, and has connected the one, infinite field of infinities not only within the numberless infinities within the Unified Field in the self-referral quality of consciousness, but also has established the relationship of the WHOLENESS of Natural Law with its diverse expressions in the ever-changing, ever-evolving diversity of the universe.

What has this done to the life of every individual and every organization in the world?

This has enlivened the relationship of the inner absolute values of life with the outer relative values of life. This has opened the door of perfection to every individual, every organization, every company, and every government.

With the introduction of the Absolute Number, the Mathematics of natural numbers has risen* to a level of fulfilment, in the same way as the discovery of the Vedic Structure of Natural Law, providing the subjective approach to science, has raised the objective approach of physical sciences to the level of fulfilment.

When the objective approach of modern science and the subjective approach of Vedic Science have created a perfect science combining both their (subjective and objective) approaches; at this time when science has become complete through both approaches—subjective and objective; at this time when the four hundred-year-

---

* We should look into the evolution of Mathematics and see how the evolution of natural numbers can
Continued on page 326 ...

old approach of modern science has evolved to the level of the subjective approach of Vedic Science, management can really be said to be a complete SCIENCE OF MANAGEMENT because management has been raised to perfection on the ground of a perfect science.

Now, when a stable state of perfection can become a living reality, it is time for the field of Mathematics to account for the precision, account for the reliable practicality, and provide a scientific foundation to this new value of management.

The Mathematics of my Absolute Number* provides a reliable basis to that system of management which can achieve any objective and place management on a stable level of fulfilment.

Continued on page 261 ...

---

* *Maharishi's Vedic Mathematics* is available as a separate publication and it is also available in *Maharishi's Absolute Theory of Management*, which provides the application of the field of WHOLENESS, the field of self-referral consciousness, to all fields of management. *Maharishi's Absolute Theory of Defence* presents the theme of management in terms of invincible defence, and offers freedom from problems and invincibility to every nation.

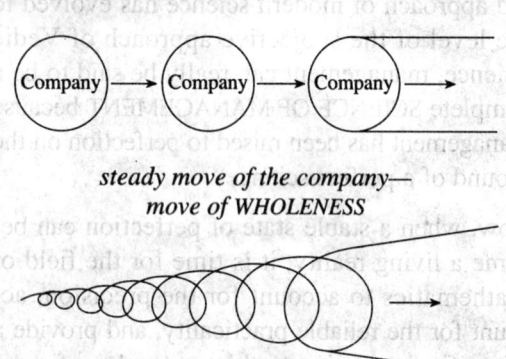

*steady move of the company—
move of WHOLENESS*

Steady growth of the company—evolving WHOLENESS—likened to ever-evolving universe.

The mathematics of the ever-evolving universe is the mathematics of the ever-evolving 'WHOLENESS'!

This surprises the precision of the Mathematics of natural numbers. This situation, faced by the science of precision (Mathematics), required another quality of Mathematics, a new feature of Mathematics. To fulfil this requirement of Mathematics, I have added the 'Absolute Number' to the field of Mathematics.

In the process of revitalizing troubled industries, we do not think of money primarily, because the obvious scarcity of money and other values that cause industry to decline is basically due to lack* of fortune. which means lack of the support of Nature—lack of support of Natural Law—lack of support of the evolutionary power of Natural Law—which shadows alertness, inhibits the flow of creative intelligence, limits innovation from within, and obstructs the nourishing influence from the environment, resulting in scarcity of all that is helpful for success.

Therefore, our primary focus is to do everything to eliminate the violation of Natural Law and gain the support of Natural Law, which will bring a new sunshine of good luck, inspiring innovation and creativity from within, and bringing a nourishing influence from all around—support of Nature from everywhere—opening a new, great gate of fortune for the revitalization

---

* Lack of fortune develops into lack of everything. Lack of fortune is lack of the lively potential of Natural Law, which means lack of Ṛk Veda, lack of Sāma
Continued on page 327 ...

of the company.

Our approach to the restoration of the company is from the most basic level of life, the level of the evolutionary power of Natural Law—the ever-evolutionary organizing power of Natural Law.

> It may be mentioned here that due to the philosophies of communism and capitalism, money gained undue importance in life; it became the primary driving force of life. The emotions and psychology of the people were just centred around earning money, and the real content of life—self-sufficiency, freedom, bliss, fulfilment, and progress in peace—was unduly shadowed by the blinding drive for money. The reality of life was shadowed and waves of living shadowed the sublime essence of life. The serene unbounded ocean of life was shadowed by the waves and even small ripples of the stressful surface of life.

We give primary importance to life and consider money as secondary importance.

In order to understand the significance and relevance of our approach to the revitalization of any company, it is necessary to understand Natural Law, the managing intelligence of Nature, which is our primary focus.

In the chapter on the origin and evolution of Natural Law (pages 35–68), Natural Law has been brought to light and has been explained as the field of all possibilities, which is available for the good luck of everyone. The sky is the limit for everyone's fortune through the knowledge and programmes of Natural Law.

The revitalization of any company, any organization, or any government is no problem today through my system of management through Natural Law.

It only requires access to the infinite or-

> ganizing power of Natural Law within the intelligence of everyone.

From the discovery of the Veda and Vedic Literature within the human physiology we know there are thirty-seven qualities of intelligence. From here we know that the holistic value of intelligence is lively in the whole physiology, and within this WHOLENESS, the organizing power of this WHOLENESS maintains holistic wakefulness in all the thirty-six values of physiology.

It is the lack of this holistic functioning of the body and mind of the individual that exposes him to the influence of stress and strain in his mind and body, and it is the stressed mind and body of the members of any company (management and employees, all together) that naturally causes the company to decline.

Thus it is clear that the revitalization of any company fundamentally calls for the restoration of the wakefulness of the organizing power of Natural Law—all the thirty-seven values of intelligence—the thirty-seven characteristic qualities of Natural Law—and their corresponding values in the physiology. (Refer to tables, pages 26–29.)

It is therefore necessary to enliven:

1. The *whole physiology* through **Ṛk Veda**;
2. its *sensory systems* through **Sāma Veda**;
3. its *processing systems* through **Yajur-Veda**;
4. its *motor systems* through **Atharva Veda**;
5. the *whole anatomy* through **Sthāpatya Veda**;
6. the *immune system and biochemistry* through **Dhanur-Veda**;
7. the *cycles and rhythms of the pacemaker cells* through **Gandharva Veda**;
8. the *autonomic ganglia* through **Shikshā**;
9. the *limbic system* through **Kalp**;
10. the *hypothalamus* through **Vyākaraṇ**;
11. the *pituitary gland* through **Nirukt**;
12. the *neurotransmitters and neurohormones* through **Chhand**;
13. the *basal ganglia, cerebral cortex, cranial nerves, and brain stem* through **Jyotish**;
14. the *thalamus* through **Nyāya**;
15. the *cerebellum* through **Vaisheshik**;

16. the *different types of neuronal activity* through **Samkhyā**;
17. the *association fibres* through **Yoga**;
18. the *twelve divisions of the central nervous system* through **Karma Mīmāmsā**;
19. the *integrated functioning of the central nervous system* through **Vedānt**;
20. the *mesodermal tissues and organs* through **Charak**;
21. the *endodermal tissues and organs* through **Sushrut**;
22. the *ectodermal tissues and organs* through **Vāgbhatt**;
23. the *cell nucleus* through **Bhāva-Prakāsh**;
24. the *cytoplasm and cytoskeleton* through **Shārngadhar**;
25. the *cell membrane* through **Mādhav Nidān**;
26. the *memory systems and reflexes* through **Smṛiti**;
27. the *great intermediate net* through **Purān**;
28. the *voluntary motor and sensory projections* through **Itihās**;
29. the *descending tracts of the central nervous system* through **Brāhmaṇa**;

30. the *fasciculi proprii* through **Āraṇyak**;
31. the *ascending tracts of the central nervous system* through **Upanishad**;
32. the *plexiform layer—horizontal communication of Layer 1 of the cerebral cortex* through **Ṛk Veda Prātishākhya**;
33. the *corticocortical fibres of Layer 2 of the cerebral cortex* through **Shukl-Yajur-Veda Prātishākhya**;
34. the *commisural and corticocortical fibres of Layer 3 of the cerebral cortex* through **Kṛishṇ-Yajur-Veda Prātishākhya (*Taittirīya*)**;
35. the *thalamocortical fibres of Layer 4 of the cerebral cortex* through **Sāma Veda Prātishākhya (*Pushpa Sūtram*)**;
36. the *cortico-striate, -tectal, -spinal fibres of Layer 5 of the cerebral cortex* through **Atharva Veda Prātishākhya**;
37. the *corticocorthalamic, corticoclaustral fibres of Layer 6 of the cerebral cortex* through **Atharva Veda Prātishākhya (*Chaturadhyāyi*)**;

It is necessary to enliven all these thirty-seven

values of Natural Law and their corresponding expressions in the physiology in order to restore the vitality of the total potential of the organizing power of Natural Law within the individual and company as a whole.

Natural Law is that irresistible, infinite power of life that makes everything always evolutionary.

Enlivenment of the infinite organizing power of Natural Law within the individual means that the inner intelligence of the body is fully awake to spontaneously function in full alliance with the intelligence of the physiology of the whole universe.

Any individual in full alliance with the universe is automatically the embodiment of the infinite organizing power of Natural Law—the lively field of all possibilities.

Here I would like to say with all emphasis that through my approach of Natural Law it is completely within the reach of any management to bless the company, or enable the company to function from the highest level of efficiency.

Everyone in the company will enjoy his full

potential of life—peace, happiness, prosperity, freedom, and fulfilment and will spontaneously contribute to the rising fortune of the company. Individuals will be free from stress and the company will be free from stress.

It will be the joy of my University of Management to introduce perfection in the corporate life of every nation.

Footnote continues from page 12 ...

unboundedness, fully awake within itself, self-referral singularity, the silent potential of all dynamism—lively silence, unmanifest pure creativity, pure field of intelligence, the field of pure knowledge, where the knower, process of knowing, and known are in their unified state—Saṁhitā (togetherness or unified state) of Ṛishi, Devatā, Chhandas—Ṛk Veda.

When human awareness settles down through Transcendental Meditation, it identifies itself with this level of reality (Ṛk Veda). In its pure wakefulness, human awareness comprehends the details of its own structure and finds that the silent value of its own nature is coexisting with the dynamic value of its own nature. The coexistence of silence and dynamism presents a picture of silence partaking of dynamism and dynamism partaking of silence.

This phenomenon of silence ceaselessly partaking of dynamism and dynamism ceaselessly partaking of silence within the structure of pure wakefulness displays dynamism in silence—displays creativity within the singularity of self-referral consciousness—which forms the basis of all the creative and evolutionary processes of the diverse universe.

This presents the nature of pure wakefulness in terms of one unified WHOLENESS, which is silence and dynamism at the same time—the structure of singularity in terms of duality.

Footnote continues ...

This presents the mechanics of singularity evolving into duality without losing its essential nature, 'singularity'. This level of intelligence, in itself, is the field of all possibilities; it is the source of creation—it displays the mechanics of creation. (Refer to pages 95–106.)

Management from this level of intelligence is the ideal of management; it is the supreme quality of management, which accomplishes automation in administration.

This is the efficiency that is developed in the management training at Maharishi University of Management.

End of this Footnote

Footnote continues from page 13 ...

founded on the ground of eternal silence; that is why natural action does not create any strain. The energy consumed in activity is simultaneously replenished from its source in eternal silence, which is pure wakefulness, absolute alertness, pure subjectivity, pure spirituality, the self-referral state of consciousness—Transcendental Consciousness on the human level of existence—easily gained through my Transcendental Meditation. This level of intelligence is the Unified Field of Natural Law.

This Unified Field of all the Laws of Nature (Saṁhitā of Ṛishi, Devatā, Chhandas—Ṛk Veda, which

Footnote continues ...

is structured in consciousness) is the field of pure knowingness, pure intelligence—the infinite, eternal state of Creative Intelligence—the lively organizing power that is available to us as *Shruti*—vibrancy of intelligence in the form of sound generated by the self-referral dynamics of consciousness—those specific sounds that construct self-referral consciousness, which have been heard by the ancient Seers in their own self-referral consciousness and are available to anyone at any time in one's own self-referral consciousness.

These sounds are the sounds that are available to us in the Veda and Vedic Literature. Through proper use of these sounds, the entire Vedic Technology—the whole engineering of creation, all the secrets of Nature's silent functioning—is available to us.

With this beautiful, practical knowledge it is possible for every government to educate its people in the science and art of living life in perfect accordance with Natural Law. Every country is now going to enjoy the infinite creativity of the organizing power of Natural Law. Heaven on Earth will be the natural result.

Modern Physics also holds that all known Laws of Nature function through the Principle of Least Action.

Classical Mechanics of a Particle:

$\int_1^2 dt\ [\ 1/2\ mv^2 - V(\mathbf{x}[t])\ ] = $ minimum

Footnote continues ...

Relativistic Motion:
$\int_{1}^{2} dt \, [-m_0 c^2 \sqrt{1 - v^2/c^2} - q(\Phi - \mathbf{v} \cdot \mathbf{A})]$ = minimum

General Relativity:
$-(c^3/16 \pi G) \int d^4x \sqrt{-g} \, R$ = minimum

Relativistic Quantum Mechanics:
$\int d^4x \, \bar{\psi} (\gamma^\mu i D_\mu - m) \psi$ = minimum

Electromagnetic Field:
$\int d^4x \, [1/4 \, F_{\mu\nu} F^{\mu\nu} - 1/2 \, F^{\mu\nu} (\partial_\mu A_\nu - \partial_\nu A_\mu)]$ = minimum

Quantum Field Theory (spin-0 field):
$\int d^4x \, \{\partial_\mu \Phi \partial^\mu \Phi^* - \mu^2 \Phi \Phi^* - \lambda (\Phi \Phi^*)^2\}$ = minimum

Superstring Theory—the Theory of the Unified Field:
$\int d^n x \, \mathcal{L}^{\text{superstring}}_{(x)}$ = minimum

In this formula, $\mathcal{L}^{\text{superstring}}_{(x)}$ symbolizes the Lagrangian of the Superstring, which represents the most compact mathematical expression of the detailed structure of the Unified Field—its symmetries, components, and self-interaction. At more superficial levels of Quantum Field Theory, this Lagrangian sequentially gives rise to the Lagrangians at the Grand Unification level, the level of Electroweak Unification, and the level of the four forces. This establishes that the Principle of Least Action is also upheld at

Continued on page 276 ...

From page 31 (1st footnote) ...

This page is for those who are familiar with the terminology of modern science.

There was a time when modern science declared that the entire creation emerged from four forces, which were thought to be fundamental. As research advanced, these so-called fundamental forces were understood in terms of one holistic Unified Field of all the Laws of Nature.

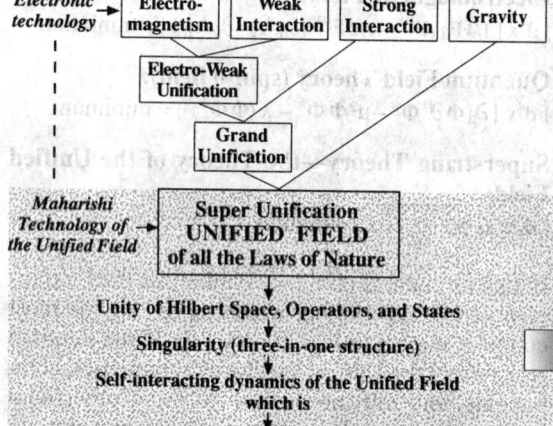

Unity of Hilbert Space, Operators, and States

Singularity (three-in-one structure)

Self-interacting dynamics of the Unified Field
which is

the dynamics of self-referral consciousness
(which according to Maharishi's Vedic Science) is the dynamics of
the three-in-one structure of Saṃhitā of Ṛṣi, Devatā, Chhandas

All the 37 areas of the Vedic Literature mentioned on the
next page are the qualities of self-referral consciousness
(the Unified Field of all the Laws of Nature)

275

From page 31 (2nd footnote) ...

▶ *This page is for those who are familiar with the terminology of Vedic Science.*

> According to Maharishi's Vedic Science, the entire classical world is the expression of the Veda—Natural Law—eternally lively within itself in terms of the self-interacting dynamics of consciousness—Samhitā (Unified State), of Ṛishi (observer), Devatā (process of observation), and Chhandas (the observed).

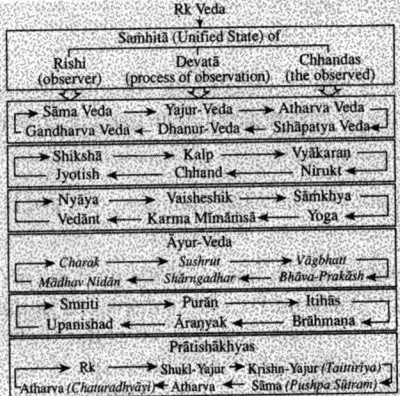

Footnote continues ...

more expressed levels of Nature.

Even without grasping the details, we see the universality of economy and effortlessness in Nature—Natural Law functions through the Principle of Least Action.

End of this Footnote

Footnote continues from page 43 ...

operator itself, at the same time it is the process of operation; that means it is the operating principle, or operating reality; it is the operator that is operating from within itself with all the tools and systems of operation lively within it—it is everything: the operator, the process of operation, and the object—it is all the three in itself.

That is why it is called the Absolute Manager on the ground of absolute managing power.

This is the vision of the evolution of Law. It is one, it is three—it is one, it is many.

This three-in-one structure of Natural Law in the language of Quantum Physics is displayed in the mathematical expression (Lagrangian) of the Unified Field in terms of the UNITY of Hilbert space, Operators, and States; according to Set Theory in Mathematics

Footnote continues ...

it is the UNITY of Set, Membership Relation, and Element; according to Chemistry it is the UNITY of Transformation Laws (Schrödinger equation), Chemical Reaction (process of reaction), and Participating Elements (reactants and products); and according to Physiology it is the UNITY of Information Units, Processing Units, and Structural Units.

This is Law—the WHOLENESS of Natural Law. This is WHOLENESS of the unified, ever-wakeful value of Law, and within the structure of Unity, the diversified structures of Law.

Each Law is endowed with WHOLENESS in its wakefulness, its unified state, and lively WHOLENESS, wakefulness, in all its diversified states.

End of this Footnote

Footnote continues from page 44 ...

people on earth who have preserved the structure of Law in its totality by memorizing and reciting the whole Constitution of the Universe, Ṛk Veda, and its structuring dynamics—the impulses of sound available in the Vedic Literature.

Law, as it evolves from its unmanifest field of WHOLENESS to all its expressions in different manifest fields, has been displayed throughout different levels of evolution. Vedic Recitation is the display of this natural evolution of Law, as it evolves from its

Footnote continues …

unmanifest state to its expressions in the Self, intellect, mind, senses, behaviour, and environment, extending to the ever-expanding universe.

Law is the functioning intelligence within everyone's physiology. Vocalizing Law in the traditional sequence of the Vedic Recitation presents the display of the sequential evolution of Law as it evolves, expressing itself from its unmanifest wholeness to its different levels of expression—from the unmanifest Self to the unmanifest intellect, mind, senses, and behaviour, extending to the whole material universe.

Vedic Recitation displays the evolution of Law from its transcendental level to the level of the senses.

Vedic Recitation is the display of the mechanics of transformation of Law as it moves from its unmanifest, transcendental value to its manifest expressions.

> In Vedic Terminology, the entire process of the evolution of Law is the move of *Atyanta-abhāva* (absolute abstraction) within itself in terms of *Anyonyābhāva* (potential dynamism)—the total dynamic potential of Law in its unmanifest state.
>
> This presents the potential of Mantra and

Footnote continues ...

> Brāhmaṇa, both aspects of Veda—the lively move of WHOLENESS—the unmanifest field of Law—the Ultimate Reality.

End of this Footnote

Footnote continues from page 52 ...

Laws of Nature (Quantum Physics) and the 'wave function of the universe' (Quantum Cosmology).

The objective approach of modern science has gone just as far as it can go. It has located the Unified Field of all the Laws of Nature, and has identified the ever-expanding universe in terms of a single wave function, as beautifully displayed in the Wheeler-DeWitt equation of Quantum Cosmology.

Now is the time for the subjective approach of Vedic Science to raise the objective approach of modern science to fulfilment.

The holistic functioning of the universe expressed by the 'wave function of the universe', derived through the objective approach of science, is expressed subjectively as the emotional awakening of Totality, where the intelligence of the individual rejoices in the blossoming of Cosmic Intelligence—*Ahaṁ Brah-*

---

* Expression of Totality in the Language of Nature, the Vedic Language.

Footnote continues ...
māsmi—I am Totality.

This is how Law, Natural Law, displays the total range of its evolution, and eternally sustains itself in the eternal move of WHOLENESS.

This is the vision of the total range of the evolution of Law, where Law eternally swings in the waves of its WHOLENESS, personified in the state of the ever-expanding universe.

At every step of evolution, every specific Law is always aligned with holistic Law, the Law of the universe, as indicated by the 'wave function of the universe', and which is expressed both objectively and subjectively by the expression:

पूर्णमदः पूर्णमिदं पूर्णात्पूर्णमुदच्यते
पूर्णस्य पूर्णमादाय पूर्णमेवावशिष्यते

*Pūrṇam adaḥ pūrṇam idaṁ pūrṇāt
pūrṇam udachyate
pūrṇasya pūrṇam ādāya pūrṇam
evāvashishyate*

(Shāntipāth, Kena Upanishad, 5.1.1)

That is full; this is full; from fullness, fullness comes out; taking fullness from fullness, what remains is fullness.

पूर्णमदः पूर्णमिदं *Pūrṇam adaḥ pūrṇam idaṁ* should be interpreted in terms of इ (I) becoming the move of अ (A). अ (A), being a continuous sound, naturally

Footnote continues ...

has the dynamics of its move within its own nature, because it moves in sameness; its existence itself is evolution.

The nature of इ (I), which is dynamism, should be lively in the nature of अ (A), which is silence continuum. This means that अ (A), the silence value of WHOLENESS, and इ (I), the dynamism value of WHOLENESS—each is WHOLENESS. This is why अ (A) is portrayed in terms of WHOLENESS, and इ (I), the nature of अ (A), is also portrayed in terms of WHOLENESS; that is why *Pūrṇam adaḥ Pūrṇam idam*.

The vision of the unity of *Prakriti* (dynamism = इ (I)) and *Purusha* (silence = अ (A)) is the vision of WHOLENESS on the move; and always being WHOLENESS, and always being on the move, its dynamism is characterized by dynamism of silence.

This is the state of absolute dynamism, which is the dynamism of Totality—the dynamism that is dynamic on the ground of silence.[*]

Any activity under the authority or influence of any

---

[*] The display of this absolute dynamism of silence, which presents the field of the Mathematics of the Absolute Number is beautifully displayed in Shiva Purāṇ or Devī Purāṇ, which account for the reality in terms of the *Prakriti* aspect of Natural Law—the dynamism of the organizing power of Natural Law.

Footnote continues ...

specific Law, whether objectively known through experimentation or subjectively known through experience, within itself is always aligned with the WHOLENESS of Law—individual Law is always in full harmony with Cosmic Law—the individual is always in harmony with the cosmos.

This is the reality of the relationship between the differentiated, individual Laws and the unified state of the WHOLENESS of Law.

If the awareness of the individual is not fully awake in the WHOLENESS of Natural Law, then it remains experientally unexposed to the natural connectedness of the specific with the non-specific, cosmic generality, or universal level of intelligence, or Law—in the Vedic Literature this loss of natural connectedness is called *Pragyāparādh*[*]—mistaken intellect.

In Cosmology, the Anthropic Principle gives us a lesson about the intercorrelation of the observer and the specific values of cosmic evolution, and thereby also shows how every specific step of evolution is in accordance with the totality.

On the superficial level, the Anthropic Principle appears as a principle that selects specificity out of

---

[*] Maharishi Āyur-Veda, in theory and practice, puts the two segregated values of intelligence together and remedies *Pragyāparādh*.

Footnote continues ...

generality and thereby deals with the mechanism that results in the emergence of the field of diversity—the field where *Pragyāparādh*, the mistaken intellect, can creep in. In its deeper value, however, the Anthropic Principle is a self-referral principle that upholds connectedness of the total cosmic evolution.

From the grand perspective of my Vedic Science, the Anthropic Principle has its climax when it is transcended, in its own dissolution, where all the specific trends of intelligence merge in their unified state—the Unified Field of Natural Law—the 'wave function of the universe'—where the observer is WHOLENESS in its unified nature; where it observes itself and experiences the Totality—*Aham Brahmāsmi*—in the Unified Field, where the diversified classical is found unified, and individuality finally wakes up to its universality—*Ayam Ātmā Brahm*—specificity is generality—Totality—WHOLENESS.

Now the world of WHOLENESS—the behaviour of WHOLENESS, unmanifest unboundedness, can be mathematically calculated, and the entire world of the behaviour of WHOLENESS can be understood in terms of the behaviour of the Absolute with the Absolute, the behaviour of the relative with the Absolute, and even the relationship of the relative with the relative in terms of the Absolute—the enormous complexity of *Karma*, which is portrayed in terms of the performance of Laws—Natural Law—and can

Footnote continues ...

be really satisfying to the intellect.

End of this Footnote

Footnote continues from page 55 ...

through the 64 different varieties of codons in the genetic language with reference to specific pieces of information (Rishi), the arrangement of information in a code (Devatā), which manifests in material structure (Chhandas)—three different languages (modes of DNA) with reference to the total potential of Nat-

---

* Ṛitam-bharā-pragyā: that quality of consciousness which sees, or comprehends, the total reality of Natural Law—the reality of Natural Law in its absolute silence and infinite dynamism.

This clear perception of the details of all possibilities—the silent dynamism of Natural Law—the total range of Natural Law displayed in the sounds of the Vedic Literature and expressed in the material structure of the universe, is open to one's awareness, and is fully awake on all levels of its expression—the Self, intellect, mind, senses, and the whole field of diversity—the field of many on the ground of Unity—many in terms of one—the state of total enlightenment, where nothing remains hidden from view, and nothing remains out of reach. This state of enlightenment is the ideal state of any management, the ideal state of any manager—the state of an all-time perfect manager.

+ These are the 64 fundamental transformations of intelligence—fundamental constituents of the self-interacting dynamics of the Veda and Vedic Literature.

Footnote continues ...

ural Law (Saṁhitā).

The triplet code of the DNA is made up of these three bases—Rishi, Devatā, Chhandas—three modes, or characteristic qualities, intrinsic to their nature, making 64 x 3 = 192 units of DNA found throughout the length of the DNA.

All the cells of the body are continually talking to each other through messengers (neuropeptides, transmitters, hormones, ...), the communication network (these 192 units) of the DNA, which correspond to the fundamental expressions of Natural Law available in the 192 *Sūkta* of Ṛk Veda—self-referral fluctuations of consciousness in the self-interacting dynamics of the Unified Field of Natural Law.

End of this Footnote

Footnote continues from page 56 ...

ever-expanding universe. This is the description of Law, the Ultimate Reality. The transcendental value of the point is the unbounded field of Law, so the nature of Law is infinitely flexible: it is totally available at a point (infinitely concentrated) and it is totally available in infinity (infinitely unbounded).

The infinitely unbounded value of Law is correlated with the infinitely concentrated value of Law at a point—everything everywhere is Law.

Footnote continues ...

The infinite flexibility of Law is beautifully portrayed in the structure of Law, which is the structure of Ṛk Veda and the entire Vedic Literature.

The entire structure of Law and its infinite flexibility is displayed in the structure of Veda—Saṁhitā of Ṛishi, Devatā, Chhandas—where three (Ṛishi, Devatā, Chhandas) emerge from one (Saṁhitā) and submerge into one with infinite speed, so that for all practical purposes Law is always emerging and submerging—it moves forward with infinite speed, it moves backwards with infinite speed—it is a great balancing power, balancing silence and dynamism in all directions at all times; it is the basis of all time, space, and causation.

This nature of Law is beautifully brought to light in my *Apaurusheya Bhāshya* (commentary) of Ṛk Veda.

End of this Footnote

Footnote continues from page 68 ...

and immediately takes that forward step to rest and recuperate its lost energy during the time that the next foot is moving.

In this example of walking, the process of evolution, or the process of moving forward is subject to the principle of rest and activity. In the case of walking, the process of rest and activity is very obvious

Footnote continues ...

because of a fairly long time of rest and a fairly long time of activity. But in the case of the process of evolution in Nature, the alternation of rest and activity happens with infinite speed because this process is taking place in the unmanifest field, which is the field of infinite correlation.

The field of infinite correlation means that every point in the field is infinitely correlated with every other point so that there is no resistance in moving from one point to the other. That is why it is called the FIELD—Unified Field of the three-in-one structure—Saṁhitā of Ṛishi, Devatā, Chhandas.

This means that the alternation of rest and activity is available in the continuation of rest and activity. This means that the process of evolution is spontaneous and continuous within the field. This is the reason why the process of evolution is spontaneous and continuous throughout the whole field of transformation, and the whole field of transformation means the infinite, unbounded field of self-referral consciousness.

Maharishi's Master Management utilizes this principle of restful dynamism—*Yogasthaḥ kuru karmāṇi (Bhagavad-Gītā, 2.48)*—and spontaneously achieves unrestricted progress.

End of this Footnote

Footnote continues from page 75 ...

Law is available in my Vedic Mathematics, the Absolute Mathematics of the Absolute Number.

It is noteworthy that the field of the Mathematics of natural numbers, as available in the world in the name of Mathematics, lacks insight into the precision of the absolute value of Natural Law displayed in the ever-expanding universe.

End of this Footnote

Footnote continues from page 90 ...

   Pūrṇam adaḥ   *Pūrṇam idam*

     अ (A)   इ (I)

   अ (A) is *full*   इ (I) is *full*

From *fullness* अ (A) emerges *fullness* इ (I)

From *fullness*   emerges   *fullness of*
of silence   *dynamism*

The move of अ (A) to इ (I) is through the sequentially evolving WHOLENESS of silence.

पूर्णमदः पूर्णमिदं पूर्णात्पूर्णमुदच्यते
पूर्णस्य पूर्णमादाय पूर्णमेवावशिष्यते

Footnote continues ...

> *Pūrṇam adaḥ pūrṇam idam*
> *pūrṇāt pūrṇam udachyate*
> *pūrṇasya pūrṇam ādāya*
> *pūrṇam evāvashishyate*
> (Shāntipāth, Kena Upanishad, 5.1.1)
> *That is full; this is full; from fullness,*
> *fullness comes out; taking fullness from*
> *fullness, what remains is fullness.*

The expression of the evolution of fullness (or wholeness) appears to be a little bit strange at first sight.

The question arises how can fullness evolve and to what can it evolve because it is already full. The word evolution here has a meaning in quality and not in quantity; it is WHOLENESS of silence that evolves into WHOLENESS of dynamism; it is qualitative evolution of one kind of WHOLENESS into another kind of WHOLENESS.

There is yet another picture of this evolution of WHOLENESS into WHOLENESS. It is highly interesting as a theory of management and that is why it is good to mention it here.

It is the holistic silence in the state of self-referral consciousness that spontaneously becomes the self-interacting dynamics of the manager's consciousness. This means that the manager is not required to make

Footnote continues ...

any effort to transform the silent quality of his self-referral consciousness into the dynamic quality of its self-interacting dynamics.

It is obvious that dynamism is latent in silence. In the potential of self-referral silence is the potential of self-interacting dynamism. This means that in order to enliven the total organizing power of Natural Law in his awareness, the manager has only to become silent—the manager has only to practise Transcendental Meditation as the basic performance of his profession—Transcendental Meditation is the tool of a perfect manager.

End of this Footnote

Footnote continues from page 95 ...
holistically awake is always successful.

The formula for success in every field of management is to develop WHOLENESS in one's conscious-

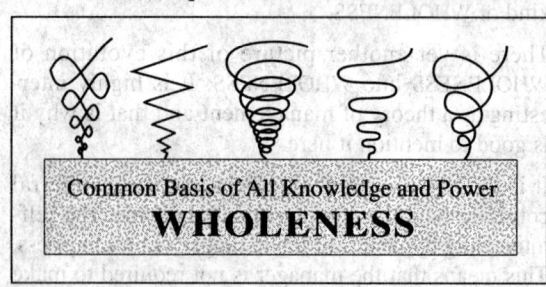

Footnote continues ...

ness—WHOLENESS is the common basis of all the different fields of knowledge and organizing power.

A Vedic Story illustrates this cardinal principle of management:

The life-promoting powers of air, water, fire, etc., were attacked by opposing negative, life-damaging forces. In their victory they started to rejoice, admiring their own individual skilful performance. A voice came saying: Remember! Victory belongs to WHOLENESS (*Brahm*)—Totality.

> Teamwork, which is an important area in modern management training, does not carry the meaning of WHOLENESS, because teamwork puts together the contributions of different members of the team, but WHOLENESS is more than the collection of parts. There are factors beyond the control of the members of the team—their state of mind and body, and innumerable influences in their personal lives that influence their alertness and their focus—which influence their performance, and without considering them the principle of teamwork does not have much relevance.
>
> Each member of the team should be holistically awake for teamwork to come within the

Footnote continues ...

range of holistic management and achieve the purpose of successful management.

Any isolated area of management should always be upheld by the management of wholeness, just as all the children are always upheld by mother.

In Nature's management, any specific, isolated performance is thoroughly infused with the holistic performance of Natural Law.

This is the total perspective of the holistic management of Natural Law, which substantiates the principle of teamwork by supporting the uniqueness of each separate quality with the unifying influence of WHOLENESS.

Maharishi University of Management educates and trains the manager to maintain a holistic quality of management by maintaining WHOLENESS—lively self-referral consciousness—Transcendental Consciousness—in his own awareness and in the awareness of all his employees, so that the total collective consciousness of the company is holistically upheld by the infinite organizing power of Natural Law, and the term 'teamwork' spontaneously realizes its total potential.

Footnote continues ...

> This is how the manager trained in Maharishi's Master Management achieves the supreme level of effectiveness in his management—WHOLENESS on the move—Totality on the move—*Brahm* on the move. This is perfect management on a par with the management of the universe.
>
> The teaching of management at Maharishi University of Management is the teaching of this level of management through Natural Law. This is Maharishi's Management — supreme management—TIMELY MANAGEMENT—suitable for all, and true for all times.

End of this Footnote

Footnote continues from page 96 ...

this three-step move of *Vāman*—three-step move of *Brahman*—three-step move of WHOLENESS—the three-step move of

Saṁhitā of Ṛishi, Devatā, Chhandas.
↓   ↓   ↓   ↓
WHOLENESS   three-step move

Three-step move of WHOLENESS is seen here in the expression

Saṁhitā of Ṛishi, Devatā, Chhandas,

Footnote continues ...

because Ṛishi is WHOLENESS, Devatā is WHOLENESS, Chhandas is WHOLENESS, and Saṁhitā is WHOLENESS—each is WHOLENESS in its own right. So the entire reality of Saṁhitā of Ṛishi, Devatā, Chhandas is a three-step move of WHOLENESS, because within the structure of Saṁhitā—unified state of Ṛishi, Devatā, Chhandas—the unified state of the observer, process of observation, and observed, the total field of diversity is included, and the structuring mechanics of Natural Law upholding the entire diversity of the universe is also included.

The vision of the mechanics of precision and order of perfect management—management of infinite diversity of the universe—is available in terms of the three-step move of WHOLENESS, Saṁhitā of Ṛishi, Devatā, Chhandas—Ṛk Veda.

End of this Footnote

Footnote continues from page 101 ...

of speech. Pronunciation of अ (A) requires full opening of the mouth.

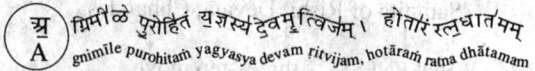

All other syllables and words require opening of the mouth in varying degrees. अ (A), which requires full opening of the mouth, is the expression of total know-

Footnote continues ...

ledge, total speech.

अ (A) is like a seed of total knowledge from where the structure of Veda emerges in sequence.

अ (A) is that total expression of consciousness which contains within itself all other qualities of consciousness.

अ (A) is the potential of all expressions of speech.

अ (A) is the expression of pure potentiality of all knowledge, the seed expression of all knowledge.

अ (A), the first letter of Ṛk Veda, is taught on the first day of school, in kindergarten, when knowledge begins—when the seed of all knowledge is planted. All the subsequently taught vowels and consonants are the quantified values of the total value of knowledge contained in अ (A).

अ (A), the expression of total speech, contains within it all other fluctuations of consciousness, all the vowels and consonants, which sequentially emerging within the structure of अ (A)—within the full opening of the mouth—constitute the structure of pure knowledge, Ṛk Veda (the totality of knowledge, Saṁhitā of Ṛishi, Devatā, Chhandas).

Ṛk Veda continues to evolve through the eternal structuring dynamics of consciousness with reference to (Ṛishi-predominant) Sāma Veda, (Devatā-predominant) Yajur-Veda, and (Chhandas-predominant)

Footnote continues ...

Atharva Veda; the Vedānga, Upānga, and Upa-Veda, etc.

The sounds of these fluctuations of consciousness (syllables, words, etc.) are the structuring mechanics—different qualities of consciousness that together constitute the structure of Ṛk Veda, and give expression to the non-expressed, self-referral state of consciousness.

Different aspects of the Vedic Literature categorize different qualities of consciousness in terms of vibrations or frequencies that are inherent in the holistic value of consciousness. These frequencies of consciousness are the expression of the intelligence that firstly gives rise to the Vedic Structure, the structure of Ṛk Veda, and continues to evolve into particles of matter and different forms of material creation.

This natural theme of evolution of consciousness starts from the holistic sound, अ (A), and evolves into the fragmented expressions of अ (A)—sounds of vowels and consonants—and in the continuing process of evolution into the forms of sound, or forms of vowels and consonants, or forms of speech, further evolving into the forms of material creation.

This is how the potential intelligence of the student of Maharishi University of Management most naturally evolves in the same sequence that creation evolves

Footnote continues ...

from the holistic sound, the first letter of Ṛk Veda, अ (A).

Through this theme of Vedic Education the entire brain physiology of the student is spontaneously trained* to function in an integrated manner—coherence is spontaneously maintained while specific quantified values of speech emerge into words, sequentially developing phrases, sentences, etc.

In order to pronounce अ (A), the total brain physiology is awake to its full potential. The pronunciation of अ (A) enlivens the whole brain physiology, and then from this level of integrated, holistic functioning, the liveliness of the total brain physiology spontaneously and effortlessly sets different parts of the brain to function and promote quantified values of अ (A), motivated by the flow of intention, inspiring different areas of the brain physiology with reference to the emotions, the five senses, etc.

The flow of the Vedic Text starts with अ (A). The pronunciation of अ (A), the holistic sound, first enlivens the whole brain physiology; every fibre of the brain wakes up; the intelligence in every fibre of the

---

* This is why the Vedic Language, which is the Language of Nature, trains the brain physiology to function spontaneously in an evolutionary direction, promoting thought and action always in accordance with Natural Law.

Footnote continues ...

brain wakes up and moves in perfect synchrony with the intelligence of every other fibre. At this stage all the brain matter, the intelligence present within every fibre of the brain, is alert on two levels: (1) holistic (total) awareness of the total intelligence of the total brain physiology, and (2) within this holistic awakening of the intelligence of the brain is the most delicate activity of each fibre of the brain matter.

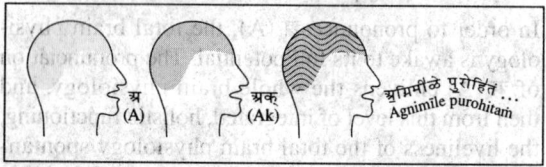

Here we have a picture just to indicate the simultaneous holistic performance of the brain and the individual performance of each fibre of the brain.

These two levels of activity of brain physiology, general and specific, characterize the pronunciation of the holistic sound, अ (A), and its sequential development into its different quantified values.

All quantified values of अ (A) are lively within this holistic and individualistic pattern of activity in the brain. Wakefulness, the basis of every level of the brain fibre, is maintained at every level of activity of each fibre of the brain.

The point to note here is that no matter what quanti-

Footnote continues ...

fied value of expression of the holistic sound, अ (A), the brain physiology will maintain the specific activity on the lively ground of holistic activity; no matter what stage of evolution of the holistic sound, अ (A), the functioning of the brain physiology remains on two levels—holistic and specific.

Pronunciation of अ ((A)—potential of total speech), spontaneously awakens and puts to performance all the innumerable neurons in the brain. The picture is that the pronunciation of अ (A) awakens all elements of the brain physiology to unite in producing the sound अ (A), and following the pronunciation of अ (A), all the elements of the brain fluctuate together with regulated back-and-forth fluctuations to collectively promote, in perfect sequence, different expressions of syllables that constitute the sequential expressions of words, sentences, etc.

Because of the absolute, orderly sequence in which the Saṁhitā flows, whenever the Vedic Mantras (Vedic Hymns) are recited, the brain activity is set in that pattern of natural, orderly flow; the brain activity is completely natural and there is no stress and strain in any part of the brain, in any fibre of the brain; the activity of every fibre automatically enlivens that level of intelligence which is at the unmanifest source of the physical existence of the brain fibres, and is the common basis of the intelligence of each brain fibre.

Footnote continues ...

This means that when the Vedic Text is correctly pronounced in its proper sequence, it stimulates all elements of the brain physiology to be fully alert and to function holistically in a coherent, orderly manner. This means that the intelligence of each fibre of the brain physiology, each specific Law of Nature, is performing its natural activity along with the holistic performance of the total brain physiology. This means that during Vedic Recitation the total potential of Natural Law is enlivened in the brain.

This means that the total potential of Natural Law, the total potential of intelligence, upholds the functioning of specific values of intelligence, specific values of Natural Law.

The holistic functioning of the human brain maintains the liveliness of the total potential of Natural Law to stimulate any and every single Law of Nature in every activity, emotion, intention, and thought.

This promotes thought spontaneously supported by the total creative potential of Natural Law.

Total potential of Natural Law is that infinite creativity of pure intelligence, pure knowledge, the Veda, which creates and maintains the whole universe in perfect order.

Maharishi University of Management offers education and training in this field of the infinite organiz-

Footnote continues ...

ing power of pure knowledge in the most systematic and scientific manner.

My Vedic Science and Technology-Based Management, being promoted through Maharishi University of Management, is the absolute level of ideal education—education to create a perfect man who will always be spontaneously supported by all the specific Laws of Nature, which spontaneously enjoy the full support of the common basis of all the Laws of Nature—the Unified Field of all the Laws of Nature, the Saṁhitā level of pure intelligence.

In this way it is clear that through daily recitation of the Vedic Literature, the brain physiology of every individual will become habituated to function in the same precise, orderly sequence in which the Saṁhitā is eternally flowing at the unmanifest basis of all creation, spontaneously promoting evolution of all life.

This habituation of the brain physiology to adopt the functioning of Natural Law spontaneously regulates the rise of every feeling, emotion, and thought in the evolutionary direction.

This culture of brain physiology is the precious gift of my Vedic theme of education.

This habitual natural functioning of the brain physiology in accordance with Natural Law provides the

Footnote continues ...

fertile ground for my Vedic Technology, which offers the 'fruit of all knowledge'—the ability to accomplish anything.

The student in his early days of study hears the sequentially evolving sounds of the Vedic Literature; his brain physiology is cultured to function in accordance with Natural Law; and with increasing familiarity with the Vedic Language and development of pure consciousness through research in consciousness, he grows in intellectual comprehension of the Vedic Text—the quantified values of the holistic sound, अ (A)—and gains familiarity with the fundamental mechanics of creation on both levels, intellectual and practical.

He is the student of Vedic Science and Technology even during his early years of study in primary and secondary school. This is how my Vedic theme of education fulfils the supreme goal of education.

My theme of imparting complete knowledge is the natural theme of evolution of knowledge available in the sequentially developing structure of Rk Veda, which is supremely orderly, absolutely perfect, and eternal—true for all time.

Maharishi University of Management provides complete education through this Vedic theme of unfoldment of knowledge.

This sequential development of knowledge presents

Footnote continues ...

the most natural, most profound, perfect theme of imparting knowledge, starting from अ (A), the first letter of Ṛk Veda.

End of this Footnote

Footnote continues from page 102 ...
Each has uniformly six divisions displaying in a systematic, sequential progression the mechanics that diversify Unity, creating Ṛishi, Devatā, and Chhandas from within Samhitā—creating the structure of Veda from the unstructured, unmanifest ocean of consciousness.

It is this EXPRESSION of the process of expression, or mechanics, or engineering, of the manifesting of the unmanifest field of intelligence that is expressed for its constituent qualities in Shikshā, Kalp, Vyākaraṇ, Nirukt, Chhand, and Jyotish, and like this all the six Upānga, the six Āyur-Veda Samhitā, the six Brāhmaṇa, and the six Prātishākhyas.

These are the Vedic Names for each cluster of a quality, which is expressed in sequential progressive expression in their divisions and their subdivisions. In this way, specific structures of Law—Natural Law—are available in the sounds of all the thirty-six well-defined, sequentially progressive structures of Natural Law.

It should be noted that it is these thirty-six modes of

Footnote continues ...

Natural Law, the internal dynamics of the unmanifest field of self-referral consciousness, that together create* the structure of Ṛk Veda.

Thus it is clear that the structure of Ṛk Veda, the structure of Natural Law, evolves through the mechanics of transformation, which are the mechanics of transformation of the holistic value of Natural Law in the unbounded, unmanifest field of consciousness.

This is the reason why it is traditionally held that Veda is not created by anyone; Veda is *Apaurusheya*—it is self-generated—it is created by itself; it moves within itself; it flows within itself; it stirs itself from within itself; and the beauty is that this move of WHOLENESS, and the resultant expressions of the holistic and specific values of Natural Law, is an all-time feature of the characteristic quality of the ocean of self-referral consciousness.

This is the reason why the Veda, as it is expressed in terms of *Apaurusheya,* is also expressed in terms of *Nitya*—eternal. So Veda, the total potential of Natural Law, the Constitution of the Universe, is eternal, self-sustained, self-created, uncreated by anyone; it is *Nitya Apaurusheya*—eternal, self-created, uncreated Veda.

---

* The move of WHOLENESS within itself (the structuring dynamics of Ṛk Veda) comes to be expressed as the Laws of Nature.

Footnote continues ...

This aspect of Natural Law has been expressed in my commentary of Ṛk Veda, *Apaurusheya Bhāshya*, which is the scientific foundation for understanding Vedic Knowledge, and which provides the technology to utilize the structure of Law in formulating one's desire in the Language of Nature, the Vedic Language, allowing Nature to spontaneously compute the process and materialize the intention.

Physics understands this phenomenon of Natural Law in terms of the Principle of Least Action, which says that Nature always chooses the simplest, most direct path to accomplish anything.

End of this Footnote

Footnote continues from page 103 ...

which presents specific sounds in sequence emerging from the self-interacting dynamics of unmanifest pure intelligence.

The Brāhmaṇa present the inner creative intelligence, the engineering, or mechanics, of structuring sound from unmanifest pure intelligence, which is heard as the Mantra of the Veda.

End of this Footnote

Footnote continues from page 108 ...

Sidhi Programme individuals grow in field independence. This means that when they are focusing sharply

Footnote continues ...

on any one area they naturally do not lose the broad comprehension of the total field of their concern; that means while managing any part, they are spontaneously managing the whole; or it can be said that they always manage the part with reference to the whole—their managing ability always manages any specific area with reference to the whole field of their concern.

This means that while attending to any one part no other parts are left out of their consideration. Their management is holistic; they have the competence to be a manager, general manager, director, or chairman of the board of directors. They are competent to undertake any great responsibility and successfully manage it without stress and strain. A greater responsibility for them is a greater joy to their personal and professional life.

[The explanation of the term 'field independence' in Vedic Terminology is for those who are familiar with the Vedic Literature and are fond of Vedic Expressions.]

In Vedic Terminology, the term 'field independence' is a term that conveys the characteristic quality of intelligence, which blossoms through the practice of Transcendentantal Meditation, and has its relevance in the word *Moksha*—freedom from boundaries.

The Vedic Expression:

Footnote continues ...

योगस्थः कुरु कर्माणि
Yogasthaḥ kuru karmāṇi
(Bhagavad-Gītā, 2.48)

(action from the unified field of self-referral consciousness—Transcendental Consciousness) is elaborated in terms of:

योगः कर्मसु कौशलम्
Yogaḥ karmasu kaushalam
(Bhagavad-Gītā, 2.50)

(performance conducted under the unifying influence of self-referral intelligence. This is 'skill in action', which is the secret of successful management), and

सहजं कर्म कौन्तेय
Sahajam karma Kaunteya
(Bhagavad-Gītā, 18.48)

(perform in a natural way without stress or strain—perform according to the evolutionary direction of Natural Law), and

प्रकृतिं स्वामवष्टभ्य विसृजामि पुनः पुनः
Prakritim swām avashṭabhya
visrijāmi punaḥ punaḥ
(Bhagavad-Gītā, 9.8)

explaining the mechanics of creation, and

यतीनां ब्रह्मा भवति सारथिः

Footnote continues …
> *Yatīnāṁ Brahmā bhavati sārathiḥ*
> (Ṛk Veda, 1.158.6)

explaining the procedure for spontaneously harnessing the infinite organizing power of Natural Law.

This Vedic Knowledge is the master key for the supreme level of management training, which will train the student of management to be the custodian of Master Management, who will display the totality of Maharishi's Master Management.

End of this Footnote

Footnote continues from page 114 …
> Administration degree.
>
> … Harvard's revamp echoes a revolution among the USA's business schools, as corporate leaders question the traditional MBA programme's relevance.
>
> In recent years, the University of Michigan, Duke University, and the Wharton School at the University of Pennsylvania have retooled their curriculums … .

End of this Footnote

Footnote continues from page 115 …
'Foreign tie-ups are being repented in haste' reports that:

Footnote continues …

In their urge to put their best foot forward in the global market, several Indian companies tied up with foreign majors. The marriages were announced with much fanfare. Now, however, in quite a few cases, disillusionment is setting in; the divorce rate is creeping up.

It started in the finance sector. ITC broke up with Peregrine after a brief honeymoon. Asian Capital Partners and Industrial Development Bank of India also decided to part ways, and S.S. Kantilal Ishwarlal (better known as SSKI) terminated its research agreement with Smith New Court.

The same story is now being repeated in other areas. Tractors major Mahindra & Mahindra (M&M) has just signed a deal with Ford Motor Co. of the U.S. to set up a joint venture to manufacture automobiles. But before Ford came into the picture, M&M had been on the verge of signing a similar deal with Chrysler (which owns a 7 per cent stake in M&M).

Chrysler's Jeep Cherokee was scheduled to be assembled in India. Other models would be added to the line-up later. So much progress had been made on the project that even advertising agencies had been asked to make presentations for the account.

Footnote continues ...

All that is off now. There is a possibility that Chrysler might sell off its stake and instead of the Jeep Cherokee one might well see the Ford Explorer rolling off the assembly lines.

Just a few days after the M&M-Ford pact was announced, another U.S. giant called it quits. AT&T and Bharti Telecom decided that their strategic alliance would not work because, as a company spokesmen put it, 'of certain irrevocable differences in the long-term business strategies' of the two companies. While it is possible that AT&T could find another partner, the likely outcome is that it will choose to go it alone.

There are several similar cases. DCM had made a foray into the automobile sector with Toyota. The Japanese have now been shown the door. Toyota is in fact one of the many Japanese concerns which seem to be finding themselves out of favour with their Indian partners.

The Japanese tie-ups have their unique problems. The rising yen has made imports (of components, etc.) much more expensive and rendered the eventual product uncompetitive on price. Besides, the somewhat strait-jacketed Japanese work ethic has not gone down too well with Indian companies.

Footnote continues ...

But what explains the other divorces? Management pundits say that it is purely a question of <u>cultural mismatch</u>.

Delegations from foreign companies (Chrysler, Ford, Volvo, Electrolux, to mention just a few) have been arriving in India in droves trying to hitch their wagon to a local manufacturer before all of them get snapped up. India is a market nobody wants to miss out on. Indian companies, on the other hand, are looking at these global giants as a stepping stone to foreign markets. With exports becoming an imperative, they know they have to get their act together soon.

Then there is the question of control. Even when the two sides have agreed in principle that there will be equal participation in equity, thorny issues crop up. The international players contend that they are much bigger, they have the technology, the cutting edge; thus, they should call the shots. The Indian companies contend that if the local market is the prime target, they are better placed.

Ford, for instance, nearly tied up with Bajaj Auto but the deal fell through over the question of management control. Royal Dutch/Shell pulled out of National Organic Chemical In-

Footnote continues ...

dustries for the same reason.

With the Indian markets catching the foreigners fancy, the marriage season is in full bloom. Tomorrow, of course, the divorce courts will be working overtime.

End of this Footnote

Footnote continues from page 122 ...

personal experiences of the impulses of Creative Intelligence, the Veda and Vedic Literature, through Maharishi's Technology of Consciousness—the Transcendental Meditation and TM-Sidhi Programme—verified by the theories of different disciplines of modern science and by the entire Vedic Literature—a practical guide to perfect management.

End of this Footnote

Footnote continues from page 123 ...

Home in which the administrators—the Laws of Nature that govern (*Devas*)—of the universe (*adhi vishwe*) reside (*nisheduh*).

ऋचो अक्षरे परमे व्योमन् ...
Richo Ak-kshare parame vyoman ...
(Rk Veda, 1.164.39)

The Hymns of the Veda are unmanifest

Footnote continues ...

> dynamism—self-interacting dynamics (*Devatā*)—the structure of dynamic intelligence—the structure of the Laws of Nature within the self-referral state of Transcendental Consciousness (*Parame vyoman*).

End of this Footnote

Footnote continues from page 171 ...

means the ability to perform action from deeper levels of silence.

With regular practice of Transcendental Meditation the individual develops Unity Consciousness, which is the ability to function from the level of silence. This is the development of mastery over Natural Law—mastery over specific Laws of Nature, which is the level of Maharishi's Master Management—automation in administration.

End of this Footnote

Footnote continues from page 178 (1st footnote) ...

> dharmasaṁsthāpanārthāya
> sambhavāmi yuge yuge
> (Bhagavad-Gītā, 4.8)
>
> *To protect the righteous and destroy the wicked, to establish Dharma firmly, I take birth age after age.*

Footnote continues ...

> Vedic Scholars will enjoy that 'I' stands for self-referral consciousness, fully alert state of *Atyantābhāva*, which is the state of absolute abstraction, the field of all transformations—the central point of transformation at every step of evolution, through which the previous state evolves into the following state.
>
> The transformation point within the nature of *Atyantābhāva* (absolute abstraction) is in terms of *Anyonyābhāva* (potential dynamism).
>
> It is enjoyable to see the 'I' as the basis of all creation and evolution. Here is the realization of :
>
> अहं ब्रह्मास्मि
> *Ahaṁ Brahmāsmi*
>   (Bṛhadāraṇyak Upaniṣad, 1.4.10)
> *I am Totality.*
>
> अयम् आत्मा ब्रह्म
> *Ayam Ātmā Brahm* (Māṇḍūkya Upaniṣad, 2)
> *This Self is Brahm.*
>
> जीवो ब्रह्मैव नापरः
> *Jīvo Brahmaiva nāparaḥ*
> *This Self, 'I', is Totality—Brahm—and none other.*

Footnote continues ...

> दूरेदृशं गृहपतिमथर्युम्
>
> *Dūre dṛishaṁ gṛihapatim atharyum*
>
> (Ṛk Veda, 7.1.1)
>
> *Far, far away I saw my Self, the indweller of my body* (Veda and Vedic Literature), *reverberating.*
>
> प्रकृतिं स्वामवष्टभ्य विसृजामि पुनः पुनः
>
> *Prakṛitiṁ swām avashṭabhya visṛijāmi punaḥ punaḥ*
>
> (Bhagavad-Gītā, 9.8)
>
> *Taking recourse to My Prakṛiti, taking recourse to My Self, 'I' create again and again*—my self-interacting dynamics promotes the sequential theme of evolution of all life.

End of this Footnote

Footnote continues from page 178 (2nd footnote)...

rasavarjaṁ raso apyasya
paraṁ dṛishtwā nivartate
(Bhagavad-Gītā, 2.59)

Having seen the Supreme, the Transcendent (bliss unbounded — the field of all intelligence and power), even the shadows of ignorance dissolve.

End of this Footnote

Footnote continues from page 178 (3rd footnote)…

all fields of life bear the testimony of the theories of all disciplines of modern science, ancient Vedic Science, and personal experience, indicating that perfection can be developed in all areas of individual and national life. (Refer to *Prachetanā—Fully Awakened Consciousness*, Maharishi Vedic University Press publication.)

End of this Footnote

Footnote continues from page 187 …

In this way the Yogic Flying technique accelerates the evolution of the individual to enlightenment—the state of fulfilment in which life is lived in full accord with Natural Law, free from suffering and problems.

The phenomenon produced by the TM-Sidhi Programme of Yogic Flying gives the experience of bliss, and generates coherence between consciousness and matter in the body. EEG studies have shown that during this phenomenon, when the body lifts up in the air, physiology and consciousness are completely integrated. This integration takes place at the level of the Unified Field of Natural Law, which has the character of infinite correlation. The impulse of coherence from this level instantly reconstructs and transforms unnatural, stressful, negative, undesirable tendencies in the brain physiology, and brain functioning becomes coherent.

Footnote continues ...

Considering this phenomenon in the light of the Unified Field Theories of modern Physics and Quantum Cosmology, we understand that the scale of Super Unification at the level of the Unified Field is associated with a fundamental phase transition in the structure of Natural Law from a diversified state to a completely unified state. The defining characteristic of such a phase transition is that the 'correlation length', which is a measure of the connectedness or correlation of different components of a system, expands to finally become infinite.

At the scale of Super Unification (Physics) all aspects of Natural Law at every point in the universe become infinitely correlated with each other.

Every single Law of Nature functions in accordance with the holistic value of Natural Law, and this is how order is maintained through the evolutionary direction of the invincible organizing power of Natural Law.

A delicate impulse at any one point in space and time can create a precipitous change throughout the entire universe. This long-range correlation explains how action on the level of the Unified Field, at the scale of Super Unification (transcendental field of intelligence), can have a profound influence that can spread anywhere and everywhere throughout the universe.

Footnote continues ...

In this way the phenomenon of coherence of groups of Yogic Flyers spreads, neutralizing the negative tendencies in the whole society. This is how modern science confirms[*] my programmes to provide perfect defence to bring invincibility to every nation.

End of this Footnote

Footnote continues from page 190 ...

coherent systems possess the ability to repel external influences, while incoherent systems are easily penetrated by disorder from outside. This principle of invincibility is clearly illustrated in Physics as the **Meissner Effect**, and in the functioning of a nation as the *Maharishi Effect*.

The significance of mentioning the Meissner Effect here is that if the national consciousness of a country is disintegrated and divided, as inevitably results from the opposition-dominated democracy of today, the country will never experience the true meaning of defence, which is invincibility; the country will always be a football of situations and circumstances.

---

[*] Confirmation from Vedic Science is available in the expression:

तत् सन्निधौ वैरत्यागः

Tat sannidhau vairatyāgaḥ (Yog-Sūtra, 2.35)
In the vicinity of coherence (Yoga), hostile tendencies are eliminated.

Footnote continues ...

Politicians will always be busy criticizing each other, and the whole purpose of administration will be lost in every generation; administration will be weak, the nation will be chaotic, and it will radiate a negative, stressful influence to all the surrounding countries.

End of this Footnote

Footnote continues from page 199 ...

the Transcendental Meditation and TM-Sidhi Programme by Professor Nicolai Lyubimov, the Russian scientist who is Professor of Neurophysiology and Experimental Neurology at the University of Moscow, and is also now the President of Maharishi Vedic University in Moscow.

Dr Lyubimov has found that those who practise Transcendental Meditation, and more so, those who practise the TM-Sidhi Programme, have access to the 'brain reserve'; that means that they have access to the total potential of Creative Intelligence, the holistic value of the brain functioning, which supports the partial values of activity of the specific parts of the brain during the processes of seeing, touching, smelling, tasting, hearing, and their corresponding actions.

This means that as the practice advances, the individual mind is increasingly in tune with the total potential of Natural Law (the Cosmic Mind) in a

Footnote continues ...

spontaneous manner, and all thought, speech, and action have the support of the infinite organizing power of Natural Law—the holistic value of Natural Law.

End of this Footnote

Footnote continues from page 204 ...

brain reserves, Abstracts of the International Symposium 'Physiological and Biochemical Basis of Brain Activity' (p. 5), St. Petersburg, Russia, June 22–24, 1994; and Mobilization of the hidden reserves of the brain, Programme Abstracts of the 2nd Russian-Swedish Symposium 'New Research in Neurobiology', Moscow, Russia, May 19–21, 1992.

End of this Footnote

Footnote continues from page 207 ...

San Diego Biomedical Symposium (1976); 'Short-Term Longitudinal Effects of the Transcendental Meditation Technique on EEG Power and Coherence', *International Journal of Neuroscience*, 14 (1981): 147–151; 'EEG Phase Coherence, Pure Consciousness, Creativity, and TM-Sidhi Experiences', *International Journal of Neuroscience*, 13 (1981): 211–217; 'Frontal EEG Coherence, H-Reflex Recovery, Concept Learning, and the TM-Sidhi Program', *International Journal of Neuroscience*, 15 (1981): 151–157; 'Enhanced Neurological Efficiency as a Result

Footnote continues ...

of the TM-Sidhi Program: Facilitation of the Paired H-Reflex', *Experimental Neurology*, 79 (1983): 77–86; and 'Factor Analysis of EEG Coherence Parameters', Fifteenth Annual Winter Conference on Brain Research, Steamboat Springs, Colorado, 28 January 1982.

End of this Footnote

Footnote continues from page 211 ...
Physiology, 221 (1971): 795–799; 'Neurophysiological and Respiratory Changes During the Practice of Relaxation Techniques,' *L'Encéphale* (The Brain), 10 (1984): 139–144; 'Breath Suspension During the Transcendental Meditation Technique', *Psychosomatic Medicine*, 44 (1982): 133–153; 'Physiological Differences Between Transcendental Meditation and Rest', *American Psychologist*, 42 (1987): 879–881; 'Adrenocortical Activity During Meditation', *Hormones and Behavior*, 10 (1978): 54–60; 'Short-term Endocrine Changes in Transcendental Meditation', *Proceedings of the Endocrine Society of Australia*, 2 (1979): Abstract 56; 'Physiological Effects of Transcendental Meditation', *Science*, 167 (1970): 1751–1754; 'Spectral Analysis of the EEG in Meditation', *Electroencephalography and Clinical Neurophysiology*, 351 (1973): 143–151; and 'Theta Bursts: An EEG Pattern in Normal Subjects Practicing the Transcendental Meditation Technique', *Electroencepha-*

Footnote continues ...

lography and Clinical Neurophysiology, 42 (1977): 397–405.

End of this Footnote

Footnote continues from page 212 ...
Medicine, 35 (1973): 341; 'Effects of the Transcendental Meditation program on stress reduction, health, and employee development: A prospective study in two occupational settings', *Anxiety, Stress and Coping: An International Journal*, 6: 242–262, 1993; 'Physiological Differences Between Transcendental Meditation and Rest', *American Psychologist*, 42 (1987): 879–881; and 'Differential Effects of Meditation Techniques on Trait Anxiety: A Meta-Analysis', *Journal of Clinical Psychology*, 45 (1989): 957–974.

End of this Footnote

Footnote continues from page 213 ...
Transcendental Meditation Technique', *Dissertations Abstracts International*, 50 (3) (1989): 1518B; 'Transcendental Meditation and Improved Performance on Intelligence-Related Measures: A Longitudinal Study', *Personality and Individual Differences*, 12 (1991): 1105–1116; 'Longitudinal Effects of the Transcendental Meditation and TM-Sidhi Program on Cognitive Ability and Cognitive Style', *Perceptual and Motor Skills*, 62 (1986): 731–738; and 'The Tran-

Footnote continues ...

scendental Meditation Programme in the College Curriculum: A Four-Year Longitudinal Study of Effects on Cognitive and Affective Functioning', *College Student Journal*, 15 (1981): 140–146.

End of this Footnote

Footnote continues from page 234 ...

and the thirty-six structuring dynamics of Ṛk Veda available in the thirty-six values of the Vedic Literature.

Together these thirty-seven qualities of intelligence constitute the total structure of Natural Law—the Constitution of the Universe—lively within the unmanifest, self-referral field of intelligence—the storehouse of total creativity—the inner intelligence of the thirty-seven structures and functions of the human physiology.

End of this Footnote

Footnote continues from page 235 ...
*My University of Management is **the** way—*
*My Vedic University is **the** way—*
*Veda is **the** way—*
*I am **the** way to perfection—*
*The 'I' within everyone is **the** way—*
*Veda within everyone is **the** way—*
*Natural Law within everyone is **the** way*

Footnote continues ...

> for everyone—
> Natural Law, the Will of God, within
> everyone is **the** way for everyone—
> I am **the** way to thee, my Lord,
> Thou art the goal in me.

End of this Footnote

Footnote continues from page 239 ...

in designing each step the manager must have the awareness of the total range of operation, like the designing of a whole production line, which requires the proper planning of completely different behavioural patterns at each step of operation.

The importance of planning is that each separate step has relevance to the total design—the designing by that intelligence which has the ability to focus sharply without losing comprehension of the whole production line—its efficiency and its purpose.

Part is all right as long as it is a joy to the whole. A wave that remains connected with the ocean can rise to any height; in the same way strategic planning is meaningful if it designs every step of progress on the basis of totality.

Strategic planning without total alertness on the part of the manager—holistic comprehension—Cosmic Consciousness—means that it is not possible for the

Footnote continues ...

manager to design a flawless, faultless production line.

Any size of production line, big or small, requires the same basis of Cosmic Consciousness, whether it concerns planning, business strategies, quality control, budgeting, or cost accounting.

End of this Footnote

Footnote continues from page 252 ...

hearing one sound involves the whole physiology and its inner intelligence. Even the sight of any one thing involves innumerable neurons and stirs innumerable values in the physiology. The whole of our intellect, mind, senses, and environment is connected with the word **management**, which simultaneously includes the management of the intellect, mind, senses, environment, and behaviour.

The handling of very many things at every moment makes management holistic, with due regard to every isolated, specific value.

It is very fortunate that the total knowledge of management—intuition, inspiration, and innovation—in theory and practice, is fully available in the Veda and Vedic Literature, which is so beautifully organized within the body of everyone, in the sequentially evolving, orderly structure of the physiology of everyone.

This is why it is easy for everyone to consciously

Footnote continues ...

access this infinite organizing power of Natural Law, which is already alert and functioning within him, and gain the ability to spontaneously handle every aspect of management through his every thought, speech, and action.

End of this Footnote

Footnote continues from page 258 ...

rise to the level of the Absolute Number, and how order in the relative world can begin to breathe the order of the world of the Absolute.

The connection between the Mathematics of natural numbers and the Mathematics of the Absolute Number is a subject of great importance, which belongs to the perfect management, or absolute management, of the wholeness of Natural Law.

I want to mention here without going into detail, that the Mathematics of natural numbers is not competent to explain the absolute precision and order that prevails in the field of perfect management, or absolute management; that is why I had to introduce the Absolute Number and evolve the Mathematics of the Absolute Number to account for the absolute precision and absolute order that perpetually prevails in the field of perfect management—the absolute management through the agency of the absolute value of Natural Law.

Footnote continues ...

This area of the Mathematics of the Absolute Number is a very fascinating field, and everyone is now going to rise to perfection through the study of the Mathematics of my Absolute Number.

In Vedic terms, this is the Mathematics of *Brahm Vidyā*, the exercise for enlightenment—the exercise to rise to mastery over Natural Law.

This whole area of knowledge is simple and is without any complexity. Even though this is the field of knowledge which is very closely concerned with management, because it is a more abstract concept, details are not being covered here.

These details are available in my Absolute Theory of Management. Here it is enough to mention that Maharishi University of Management is presenting that supreme level of perfection, which has at its basis the absolute precision of the Mathematics of the Absolute Number.

End of this Footnote

Footnote continues from page 261 ...
Veda, lack of Yajur-Veda, lack of Atharva Veda, lack of Sthāpatya Veda, lack of Dhanur-Veda, and lack of Gandharva Veda; lack of Shiksha, lack of Kalp, lack of Vyākaraṇ, lack of Nirukt, lack of Chhand, and lack of Jyotish; lack of Nyāya, lack of Vaisheshik, lack

Footnote continues ...

of Sāṁkhya, lack of Yoga, lack of Karma Mīmāṁsā, and lack of Vedānt; lack of all the thirty-six qualities of the holistic value of Natural Law; lack of the holistic value of Natural Law; lack of the move of WHOLENESS, the move of Natural Law; lack of wakefulness of the structuring dynamics of Ṛk Veda—lack of the structuring dynamics of Natural Law.

This lack of the structuring dynamics of Natural Law disallows Natural Law to appear. When there is a lack of the structuring dynamics of Law then, it is obvious that there is no structure of Law—Law is unavailable—there is nothing that can happen. This means that there is nothing precise and orderly that can happen, which means that precision and order are unavailable, the move of WHOLENESS is unavailable, perfection of management is unavailable, support of Nature is unavailable—randomness, entropy, disorder, and chaos can be the only result.

In order to visualize the source of disorder, we should look into the reality of the organizing power of Natural Law, as described in the Sāṁkhya system of management in the Vedic Literature; we should look into the reality of WHOLENESS on the move.

We have already covered the move of WHOLE-

Footnote continues ...

NESS in terms of the move of silence — dynamism*of silence—the dynamism nature of silence. This reality of the structure of management at the basis of all creation and evolution is described in the Vedic Terminology as a 'joint venture' of the two qualities inherent in Natural Law—silence and dynamism—*Prakṛiti* (eternal dynamism) and *Puruṣha* (eternal silence). The term 'team work' in management has its basis in this dynamism of silence—*Prakṛiti* of *Puruṣha*.

It is important to note here that it is the quality of silent dynamism that constitutes the organizing power of Natural Law. Ṛk Veda says that the ability to utilize this organizing power of Natural Law—to set in motion the infinite organizing power on the level of individual life—is available to anyone whose awareness is awake in this quality of dynamic silence—self-referral silence—self-referral dynamic silence—silence of Transcendental Consciousness—

यतीनां ब्रह्मा भवति सारथिः
Yatīnāṁ Brahmā bhavati sārathiḥ
(*Ṛk Veda, 1.158.6*)

---

* Refer to pages 85–106.

Footnote continues ...

> *For those established in self-referral consciousness, the infinite organizing power of the Creator becomes the charioteer of all action.*
>
> Practically it is the phenomenon of Yogic Flying, which is basically the phenomenon of self-referral consciousness demonstrating its corresponding state of physiology—the demonstration of '*Yati*'—the demonstration of Totality on the move—WHOLENESS on the move—infinite organizing power on the move — total Creative Intelligence on the move—Cosmic Intelligence on the move—which means 'that which is the move of WHOLENESS'—that quality of intelligence which spontaneously engages the infinite organizing power of Natural Law, silent *Purusha* and dynamic *Prakṛiti* (dynamic silence), and actualizes *Brahmā bhavati sārathiḥ*—automation in the actualization of desire.

End of the Last Footnote

Enlightenment and Fulfilment in Management

Enlightenment is that state of human awareness in which 'WHOLENESS moves'[*] and spontaneously achieves the supreme goal of management — fulfilment to all concerned — Maharishi's Master Management—automation in administration—the IDEAL of business management and public administration—the goal of Maharishi University of Management.

The principles and programmes are in our hands; those who want to derive the benefits are welcome to take this knowledge and not only free themselves from problems on a permanent basis, but enjoy fulfilling progress now, and for all future.

Maharishi University of Management has a 'Department of Solutions' for handling problems of management. Our speciality is in introducing Natural Law in the field of management.

Any management (any company or any govern-

---

[*] Refer to page 95.

ment) that is facing any kind of problem today can be turned around to enjoy success tomorrow. It depends upon the speed of their response. From our side we are ready to eliminate problems and produce the desired results in a minimum amount of time for any government or any industry or any company.

We want to emphasize that in this scientific age there is nothing that cannot be achieved through the support of Natural Law—nothing is impossible if one takes recourse to the Unified Field of Natural Law, the Quantum Field of Natural Law, where WHOLENESS is on the move at all times.

If there are problems anywhere, they are always the problems of management. This means that management must be improved. Arguments and logic to establish that problems have their origin somewhere outside the realm of the manager himself is a poor excuse; the fact is that problems are only due to inadequate training in management.

Maharishi University of Management offers perfect management through the move of WHOLE-

NESS—through the managing intelligence of Nature—which leaves nothing out of the grip of management. It is our delight to offer this level of perfection to any system of management in the world.

Our offer of excellence in management is simple, comprehensive, and rewarding in every way; it is the result of thirty-eight years of success around the world, supported by a large body of scientific research, which has been documented by the personal experience of millions of people throughout the world, and upheld by the principles and programmes of the objective approach of modern science and the subjective approach of ancient Vedic Science.

With this there is a good reason for everyone to believe that Maharishi's Master Management will free management in the world from problems and create a new enlightened level of intelligent leadership to guide all management in the direction of success.

In 1973, I addressed[*] the 28th Annual Conference of the American Association for Higher Educa-

---

[*] 13 March 1973.

tion in Chicago with the desire to introduce ideal education in America. With the establishment of Maharishi Vedic Universities and Maharishi Āyur-Veda Universities in many states in America, and now with the programme to establish Maharishi Universities of Management, and Maharishi Schools and Colleges throughout the U.S.A., my desire to provide ideal education in the most creative country in the world has been fulfilled.

When I accepted[*] 'The Hope' Award in 1970, I accepted the challenge to fulfil the hope of the world that was placed in me; I was happy to find that the demand was in the same direction in which I was naturally moving. Now, having established Maharishi University of Management, I feel that I have fulfilled that hope by establishing an organization which can eliminate problems and create an enlightened, happy society.

---

[*] The Professions and Finance Division of the Merchants Club for the City of Hope presented 'The Hope' Award to Maharishi 'who seeks to uplift the human spirit and combat despair in our troubled world'.

We will count ourselves successful only when the problems of today's world are substantially reduced and eventually eliminated; the educational institutions of every country are capable of managing education successfully, producing fully developed, enlightened citizens; those responsible for managing health are capable of protecting society from suffering; management in business and industry is capable of enlivening the full creative potential of their concerns, enjoying success without stress; governments are able to administer society without problems, satisfy everyone, and realize the beautiful goals of their constitutions—and management everywhere is fulfilling to all, in the direction of Heaven on Earth.

Invitation

Maharishi University of Management will welcome those responsible for education, directors of industries, Ministers of governmental organizations, and Mayors to apply to Maharishi University of Management in Chicago for courses and seminars to be held in their country according to their convenience.

Maharishi's Achievements
*A Glimpse of Thirty-Eight
Years Around the World
1957–1995*

HIS HOLINESS MAHARISHI MAHESH YOGI, founder of Transcendental Meditation and the world-wide Spiritual Regeneration Movement (1957), introduced research in the field of consciousness and brought to light seven states of consciousness (1957–1967); created a new science—the Science of Consciousness, the Science of Creative Intelligence—and trained 2,000 teachers of this science (1972) [by now 40,000]; discovered the Constitution of the Universe—the lively potential of Natural Law—in Ṛk Veda, and discovered the structuring dynamics of Ṛk Veda in the entire Vedic Literature (1975); celebrated the Dawn of the Age of Enlightenment on the basis of the discovery of the *Maharishi Effect* (1975); created a World Government for the Age of Enlightenment with its sovereignty in the domain of consciousness and authority in the invincible power of Natural Law (1976); introduced the TM-Sidhi Programme and the experience of bubbling bliss in Yogic Flying to create supreme mind-body co-ordination in the individual and coherence in world consciousness (1976); formulated Maharishi's Absolute Theory of Government, Maharishi's Absolute Theory of Education, Maharishi's Absolute Theory of Defence, Maharishi's Absolute Theory of Health, Maharishi's Absolute Theory of Economy, Maharishi's Absolute Theory of Law and Order, and Maharishi's Absolute Theory of Rehabilitation to raise every area of life to perfection (1977); brought to light the commentary of Ṛk Veda, *Apaurusheya Bhāshya,* as the self-generating, self-perpetuating structure of consciousness (1980); organized the centuries-old scattered Vedic Literature as the literature of a perfect science—Maharishi's Vedic Science and Technology (1981); brought to light the full potential of Āyur-Veda, Gandharva Veda, Dhanur-Veda, Sthāpatya Veda, and Jyotish to create a disease-free and problem-free family of nations (1985); formulated the Master Plan to Create Heaven on Earth for the reconstruction of the whole world, inner and outer (1988); brought to light Supreme Political Science, introduced automation in administration, and inspired the formation of a new political party, the Natural Law

Party, in countries throughout the world (1992); inaugurated Global *Rām Rāj*—Global Administration through Natural Law (1993); now establishing Maharishi Vedic Universities, Maharishi Āyur-Veda Universities, and Maharishi Universities of Management throughout the world to offer mastery over Natural Law to every individual and to perpetuate life in accordance with Natural Law—perfection in every profession—and create Natural Law-based problem-free government in every country—governments with the ability to prevent problems (1993–1995). Discovery of the Veda and Vedic Literature in the human physiology has finally established the grand unity of all material diversity of creation, of all sciences, and of all religions (last quarter 1993). This has heralded the Dawn of the Vedic Civilization, civilization based on pure knowledge and the infinite organizing power of Natural Law—life according to Natural Law—where no one will suffer; all will enjoy the eternal glory of God—Heaven on Earth.

In 1994, Maharishi introduced programmes for prevention in the fields of health and security, to create healthy national life and an invincible armour of defence for the nation, by introducing new prevention-oriented programmes of Maharishi Āyur-Veda for perfect health, and by introducing the programmes for a PREVENTION WING in the military of every country to disallow the birth of an enemy just by training a small percentage of the military in the Vedic Technology of Defence—Transcendental Meditation, the TM-Sidhi Programme, and Yogic Flying.

This second quarter of 1995 is ready to unfold still greater achievements—invincibility and the establishment of permanent world peace—the foundation of Heaven on Earth.

341

Cosmic Intelligence, absolute intelligence of Natural Law, displaying its infinite managing power in the orderly administration of the ever-evolving, ever-expanding universe.

' the Management of the Universe
ıt on all levels of life on earth.

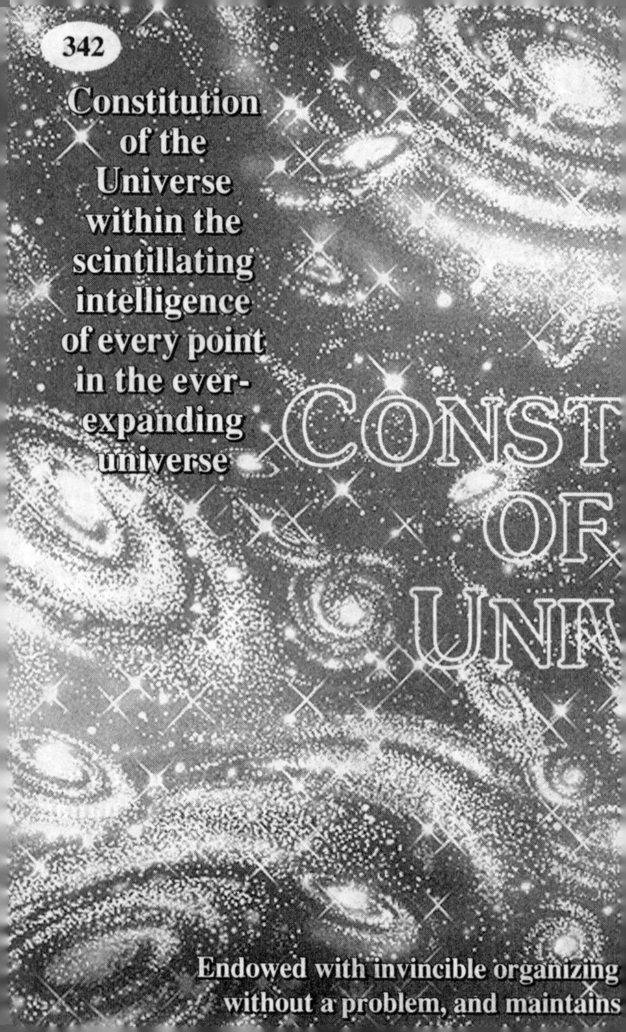

342

Constitution of the Universe within the scintillating intelligence of every point in the ever-expanding universe

CONST
OF
UNI

Endowed with invincible organizing
without a problem, and maintains

The Constitution of the Universe, the source of all the Laws of Nature—the managing intelligence of the universe—will now be utilized to bring fulfilment to management on all levels of life in every country.

, Natural Law manages the universe
ation in Cosmic Administration.

Maharishi's Master Management comes from Maharishi Consciousness—fully awake, fully alert intelligence of self-referral consciousness—the fully alert, fully awake intelligence within every grain of creation and within the universe as a whole.

WHOLENESS

The colourful flags of every sovereign nation, flying high, welcoming the move of WHOLENESS—the nourishing take-over by the Government of Nature.

Management in every country will now enjoy the nourishing, harmonizing, and purifying organizing power of Natural Law.

347

THE MOVE

The light of WHOLENESS
on the globe

1995

Notes	Page

Notes	Page

Notes	Page

Notes	Page

Maharishi University of Management upholds Maharishi's Absolute Theory of Management, which is complemented by:

- Maharishi's Absolute Theory of Education
- Maharishi's Absolute Theory of Health
- Maharishi's Absolute Theory of Government
- Maharishi's Absolute Theory of Defence
- Maharishi's Absolute Theory of Rehabilitation
- Maharishi's Absolute Theory of Law and Order
- Maharishi's Absolute Theory of Economy

These are available as separate publications.

Maharishi University
of Management
Holland, U.S.A., Russia.